Cambridge Elements

Elements in Music Since 1945
edited by
Mervyn Cooke
University of Nottingham

UNDERSTANDING STOCKHAUSEN

Robin Maconie
Independent Scholar

Shaftesbury Road, Cambridge CB2 8EA, United Kingdom

One Liberty Plaza, 20th Floor, New York, NY 10006, USA

477 Williamstown Road, Port Melbourne, VIC 3207, Australia

314–321, 3rd Floor, Plot 3, Splendor Forum, Jasola District Centre, New Delhi – 110025, India

103 Penang Road, #05–06/07, Visioncrest Commercial, Singapore 238467

Cambridge University Press is part of Cambridge University Press & Assessment, a department of the University of Cambridge.

We share the University's mission to contribute to society through the pursuit of education, learning and research at the highest international levels of excellence.

www.cambridge.org
Information on this title: www.cambridge.org/9781009294294

DOI: 10.1017/9781009294263

First published 2022

A catalogue record for this publication is available from the British Library.

ISBN 978-1-009-29429-4 Paperback
ISSN 2632-7791 (online)
ISSN 2632-7783 (print)

Understanding Stockhausen

Elements in Music Since 1945

DOI: 10.1017/9781009294263
First published online: November 2022

Robin Maconie
Independent Scholar

Author for correspondence: Robin Maconie, maconie@xtra.co.nz

Abstract: This collection of essays addresses technical developments in telecommunications and sound recording that have guided the direction of musical aesthetics in the post-1950 era. Such information is readily available online but may appear counterintuitive to many who find its priorities difficult to grasp from a musical perspective. The author hopes to draw attention to the place of ideas of communication and flight in Western tradition. This Element begins with Varèse and his 'noble noise', traverses the arrival of Information Theory and its influence, examples of early computer music, and ends with a defence of the sublime logic of Stockhausen's singing helicopters and tornados.

Keywords: Stockhausen, *Helicopter String Quartet*, *Ionisation*, *Cosmic Pulses*, RCA synthesizer

ISBNs: 9781009294294 (PB), 9781009294263 (OC)
ISSNs: 2632-7791 (online), 2632-7783 (print)

Contents

1 Information Theory

Tucked into the final chapter of Part One of Louise Varèse's biography of her husband is the intriguing paragraph:

> After spending a day talking with an electrical engineer of the Bell Telephone Laboratory of Pennsylvania he wrote: 'Went to Philadelphia for the whole day yesterday to work. It was wonderful. Sooner or later I'll get what I want. Weyl is extremely knowledgeable and intelligent'. That fall Varèse would meet Harvey Fletcher, director of physical research at Western Electric in New York, and for a while [Varèse's] optimism [for support for electroacoustic music research] seemed justified.[1]

Varèse sought Harvey Fletcher's support in persuading Western Electric to fund research in the development of an electronic instrument of a type conceived by Ferruccio Busoni, based on the Dynamophone of Thaddeus Cahill, with which to explore new realms of harmony. 'My objectives,' Varèse wrote, 'are two-fold: acoustical research in the interest of pure music and the working out and application of certain results for the improvement of the Sound Film – with other ramifications, radio, etc.'[2] The early 1930s was a period of active production of electronic musical instruments, including the Hammond organ and electric piano. In 1928 RCA acquired the rights to the theremin, put into production under the name RCA Thereminvox. Claire Reis, of the League of Composers, recalled that Alfred Norton Goldsmith, vice president and general manager at RCA, was also 'extremely interested in the new field which he felt was being opened up for electronics in music'.[3] Harvey Fletcher was the director of physical research at Western Electric, whose premises were located a short walk away from Varèse's home in New York. Fletcher had oversight of the firm's collaboration with Leopold Stokowski and the Philadelphia Orchestra, culminating in an historic experimental landline transmission, on 27 April 1933, of a concert programme from the Philadelphia Academy of Music to a powerful speaker system mounted on the concert platform at Washington's much larger Constitution Hall.

Fletcher's response to Varèse's overtures had been friendly, no doubt padded out with supportive press releases on the company's research activities, including the vocoder. In 1928, investigatory work on Varèse's project began, only to be discontinued following the Stock Market Crash of 1929. Varèse determined to keep pushing. On 6 March 1933, a month before the Constitution Hall

[1] Louise Varèse, *Varèse: A Looking-Glass Diary, Volume I: 1883–1928* (London, 1973), pp. 260–1, 277–8.

[2] Fernand Ouellette, *Edgard Varèse: A Musical Biography* trans. Derek Coltman (London, 1974), pp. 128–31.

[3] Claire Reis, *Composers, Conductors, and Critics* (New York, 1955), pp. 114–31.

experimental transmission, Nicolas Slonimsky conducted the premiere of Varèse's *Ionisation* for thirteen percussionists and about forty instruments, tuned and untuned, including two sirens, in New York's Carnegie Chapter Hall. *Ionisation* deserves to be recognized as the composer's attempt to make music in the terms of a vocoder, or graduated filter bank, replacing the traditional orchestra by an ensemble largely of percussion instruments comprising a scale of noise bandwidths or resonances of varying degrees of colour or brightness. Such a stratified, low-resolution kind of music appeared designed to be transmitted across the world by telegraph cable, as the vocoder had originally been designed to transmit speech internationally by cable. Listeners were impressed at the composer's resourcefulness in constructing an orchestra of noises instead of the exact pitches of conventional music. But no one could quite figure out Varèse's intention. Hearing *Ionisation* on disc for the first time in 1955 prompted a visceral reaction in fourteen-year-old Frank Zappa. More recently Boulez approached the piece, as he did all of Varèse's music, like a surgeon, operating delicately from behind a mask, while confessing to reporters that the basis of Varèse's aesthetic eluded him. A tribute essay by Milton Babbitt, 'Edgar Varèse: A Few Observations of His Music', included these remarks on *Octandre* (1923):

> It is clear that, for Varèse, the invariant aspect of an instrument, in some important sense, the timbre of the instrument, is to be identified with its formant, that fixed, 'amplificatory' resonance region of an instrument, which operates upon the spectrum of the input sound, resonating, according to the characteristics of the formant region, those partials whose frequencies fall in this region, and – thereby – attenuating those whose frequencies do not.
> . . . Crescendi . . . produce . . . a continuation of the number, relations, and densities of the partials of the total spectrum.[4]

Viewed strictly as a compilation of phrases from an acoustics textbook, Babbitt may be correct; but to a lay reader the above description is all but impenetrable, the author clearly not understanding that the process he is describing is a version of what happens acoustically inside the vocal cavity when a person speaks. Concerning *Ionisation*, Odile Vivier observed with amiable perspicacity that in the composer's hands the various percussion instruments functioned effectively as filtered resonances:

> The piano also is only utilized for resonance: crisp, sharp attacks, which are allowed to linger for a certain duration. Here, as later in *Déserts*, we see how Varèse draws inspiration from the 'theory of vowels' of Helmholtz. The large

[4] Milton Babbitt, 'Edgard Varèse: A Few Observations of his Music' (1965). In Stephen Peles et al. eds., *Collected Essays* (Princeton, NJ, 2011), p. 218.

> aggregations of notes are not really *tone clusters*, the score gives no indication that they should be played that way at all, with the palm of the hand, fist, or forearm.[5]

Between the wars, young American composers travelled to Paris to study with Nadia Boulanger. Mlle Boulanger's most admired gift as a teacher was her ability to intuit the direction of a composer's thought. 'I am convinced', wrote Aaron Copland,

> that it is Mademoiselle Boulanger's perceptivity as a musician that is at the core of her teaching. She is able to grasp the still-uncertain contours of an incomplete sketch, examine it, and *foretell the probable and possible ways in which it may be developed*. . . . At the period when I was her pupil she had but one all-embracing principle, namely, the desirability of aiming first and foremost at the creation of what she called '*la grande ligne*' – the long line in music.[6]

If Babbitt's remarks on *Octandre* appear to have been drawn piecemeal from a textbook on acoustics, and many of Cage's lectures assembled seemingly at random from a variety of sources, there is reason to suppose that among Nadia Boulanger's most valued skills was her ability to pronounce, on the basis of a few random sketches, what a young pupil was thinking about and how those ideas might be put together and developed towards a larger form. Admitted Copland admiringly, 'she was able to extract from a composer of two-page songs and three-page piano pieces a full-sized ballet lasting thirty-five minutes'. What Mlle Boulanger understood by the long line is conveyed with particular eloquence by the soaring first movement theme of Stravinsky's *Ode* (1943) in memory of Natalie Koussevitsky; however what Copland understood by *la grande ligne* is perhaps more aptly conveyed by his sentence cited earlier, a construction padded out with superfluous material and three times as long as its factual content requires. Taking its author literally, a long line is a sign of culture: longwinded, self-conscious, short of content, and dressed with redundancy. A long line, it implies, is designed to sound impressive, not for coherence, neither to explain, develop, nor to transfer data efficiently.

In the May 1954 issue of *MAD*, an early number of the satirical magazine, editor Harvey Kurtzman experimented with the horror comic genre by reprinting a formulaic three-page strip by artist Jack Davis, 'Murder the Husband!' extracted from the EC publisher's archive in its original form, alongside a parody version, retitled 'Murder the Story!'. The parody version preserved

---

[5] Odile Vivier, *Varèse* (Paris, 1973), pp. 95–6. *See also* Hermann Helmholtz, *On the Sensations of Tone* (New York, 1954), pp. 103–19.

[6] Aaron Copland, *Copland on Music* (London, 1961), pp. 89–90.

the art work, but its accompanying text and dialogue were rearranged, subverted, and on occasion entirely replaced, to include incongruous lines from Doris Day songs, and cut-outs of alien text in Japanese, German, Greek, Russian, and Hebrew.[7]

The primary purpose of the experiment was to amuse, but the subtext of Kurtzman's exercise was to ask how the reader would be expected to interpret a story in which the visual content remained coherent, but the word content – both 'narrative' and 'speech' – was significantly degraded. This in fact was an approach adopted by US codebreaking specialists during and after World War II. Suppose we treat the actual text as superfluous content, they reasoned, and consider the meaning of an intercepted message from a different perspective, or set of factors: who may have sent the message and to whom; where it originated and was received; at what time; how long was the message; what names, if any, were mentioned; and so on.

Similarly playful tactics were applied by Spike Jones and his City Slickers during and after the war to familiar items of classical music. In these parodies the musical outlines and harmonies of an original composition were largely preserved, but their pretensions punctured and subverted by the substitution of incongruous or disruptive sound effects: a pistol shot, a gargling voice. In the best of Spike Jones, the classical 'long line' is preserved, and the value of the emotional gesture respected, but applied to insinuate a logical connection in an audio montage or *Merzbild* composed in the style of Kurt Schwitters, and consisting in large part of discarded, instantly recognizable sound materials from the world of radio – a genre the humourless French would attempt after the war to elevate into an art form.

In November 1942, Alan Turing arrived in New York on a prearranged mission to discuss the setting up of a secure telephone line between Washington and London. The meeting did not go as planned. Turing, whose expertise lay in text decryption, had expected to meet up with 'Potter' at Bell Laboratories. Ralph K. Potter was the leader of a research team investigating the potential of a speech encryption system, based on the vocoder. Upon arrival in New York, Turing found himself detained on Ellis Island, temporarily prevented from observing anything to do with speech secrecy. Released from detention, instead of meeting with Potter, Turing passed the time in conversation with Claude Shannon in the Bell Labs cafeteria. Shannon was a specialist in statistical analysis, not speech recognition. He knew of Turing's reputation and was almost certainly briefed to find out as much as he could about what Turing

[7] Martia Reidelback, *Completely MAD: A History of the Comic Book and Magazine* (Boston, MA, 1991), pp. 25–6.

knew about German text transmissions, while having little knowledge himself to divulge, even inadvertently, of voice encryption.

Both US and British allies were anxious to develop operational memories to store data alongside existing computing devices. It was a matter of interest to the Americans to know if existing British developments in data processing incorporated storage mechanisms that could be adapted to real-time speech processing. There were suspicions and rivalries on both sides. Shannon would later claim that the pair had not discussed cryptography at all, and that he had no knowledge of the Enigma machine. Among topics he admitted the pair did talk about were the possibilities of computer intelligence, chess-playing machines, and how to model human reasoning – topics of relevance to the prospect of realizing Turing's Universal Computing Engine with the aid of Shannon's high-speed electrical relays.[8]

Turing had been despatched to New York to meet Potter to discuss the proposed telephone link. The vocoder team at Bell Labs was rumoured to be working on a Basic English register or memory store of phonemes corresponding to an alphabet of speech sounds from which spoken messages could be reassembled. These speech sounds could be notated graphically in simplified form. Visible speech had developed from Homer Dudley's original vocoder, a voice compression mechanism designed for the transmission of telephone messages by cable, to which a visual display had subsequently been attached allowing an operator to observe the characteristic resonances of the speech signal. To accompany the equipment in its revised form a user's manual was being compiled to assist speech therapists and allow the hearing impaired to interpret speech by sight from continuously updated resonance patterns of filtered speech displayed as slow-moving tongues of fire on a cathode tube screen. Following urgent inquiries into whether the elements of such an index of phonemic units could be freely combined to synthesize speech, it had emerged that for such an application to succeed would require enlarging the database to include an additional and potentially limitless register of transitional sounds in order to reproduce properly liaised phrases and sentences of coherent speech. While not meaningful in isolation, these interpolations were essential for ease of understanding, to maintain a sense of continuity, and assist in conveying an appearance of personality and intentionality.

Adopting a mechanism similar to the tone-controlled multi-channel audio projection system of RCA Fantasound, the vocoder employed a bank of ten narrow-pass filters spaced at one-third octave intervals allowing the fluctuations in intensity of telephone speech to be compressed into a narrow cluster of

[8] Jack Copeland, *The Turing Guide* (Oxford, 2017), pp. 183–7.

amplitude modulated layers for transmission by cable and subsequent expansion and recovery at the destination with the aid of suitable resonance channels. 'The signal produced by each filter was subsequently amplitude-modulated by its corresponding low-frequency signal and the ten channels were combined to reconstitute the speech, in an attempt to mimic the dynamic acoustic resonances of the human mouth, tongue, nose, and throat.'[9] Taking his cue from Dudley's earlier patent, in order to further reduce bandwidth Potter had suggested reserving the high-frequency resonance components – the region of noises representing consonants – for separate processing as off-on channels rather than continuously modulated signals. As a result, unsurprisingly, 'the [reproduced] speech was badly mutilated'. It is possible that this embarrassing outcome and Shannon's hasty recruitment as a noise reduction or 'smoothing filter' consultant may have contributed to the delay in proceeding with Turing's meeting, and the unexpected replacement of Potter by Claude Shannon, as well as explaining Shannon's absence of preparation for substantive discussion.

On being advised of the purpose of Turing's visit, Potter would have had to admit that analogue speech is not reducible to a succession of discrete states – or rather, that it would require the interpolation of transitional states such as artificial diphthongs to reproduce a speech signal to an acceptable standard of intelligibility – an admission explaining why Potter's originally scheduled meeting with Turing was cancelled. The visible speech team subsequently reported:

> It would be convenient for reading if each sound always had only one pattern, but as we combine sounds into syllables and words in connected speech, one sound influences and is changed or influenced by the sound with which it is combined. . . . The patterns indicate that the articulators spend about as much time in the transitional movements as they spend in the characteristic or steady state positions. . . . The basis of how sounds influence each other is in the way the resonating cavities change in shape and size as we say one sound after another in pronouncing words. . . . All sounds are changed to some extent by the sounds that come before and after them.[10]

In Britain, Turing had been tasked with decryption by pattern recognition of German naval telegraph transmissions received in encrypted, but coherent and reversible, text created by a process similar to one in which typewritten messages were repeatedly shuffled from QWERTY keyboard to non-QWERTY keyboard, the pattern of keystrokes remaining the same. As part of a broader

[9] David Kahn, 'Cryptology and the origins of spread spectrum'. *IEEE Spectrum* (September 1984), https://spectrum.ieee.org, 24 September 2018.

[10] Ralph J. Potter, George A. Kopp, and Harriet Green Kopp, *Visible Speech* (New York, 1966), pp. 38–9.

inquiry into the fundamental units of American English speech, Potter and his team looked briefly into the possibility of applying visible speech protocols to speech synthesis and voice recognition. The necessarily degraded quality of vocoder transmissions did not help matters. The methodological weakness of German text encryption was that underneath all the disguises lay coherent, highly structured operational instructions delivered in a form designed to be decrypted urgently by specialist naval radio officers for immediate execution. The corresponding weakness of the proposed US telephone link between Washington and London was that underneath the noise the original speech would remain connected and correctly ordered. By the time Turing arrived in New York it may already have been decided that the original basis on which the encrypted telephone link had been proposed was theoretically flawed and practically unworkable. The question then would be how to save face, and after that, how to arrive at a system that worked.

As a researcher at MIT, Shannon had assisted in the design of an improved and extremely fast version of a modular control system for the Vannevar Bush differential analyser, employing electrical circuits and switches. This was an analogue computer.

> Shannon's master's thesis 'A Symbolic Analysis of Relay and Switching Circuits' was finished in the fall of 1937. It includes the statement 'any circuit is represented by a set of equations. . . . This calculus is shown to be exactly analogous to the calculus of propositions used in the symbolic study of logic'. . . . That same year, the British mathematician Alan Turing . . . had proven that any solvable mathematical problem could, in principle, be solved by machine.[11]

Subsequently, Shannon had practised on an abandoned eugenics database to refine techniques and applications of data storage and retrieval. The deconstruction of personal data into multiple categories, assigning each a value from which a statistical profile could be generated, and then developing means of evaluating conditions or tendencies in select groups or combinations of attributes at electric speeds, clearly had potential for pattern recognition applications in encrypted telegraph messages of limited size amounting to arrangements of little more than twenty-six letters of the alphabet, ten numerals, and one space. Statistical analysis allowed for filtered searching of a population database by one or more characteristic features or factors.

From a musical perspective, the approach applied by Shannon is clearly serial in implication. The task of defining a population as a register of categories and

[11] Jimmy Soni and Rob Goodman, *A Mind at Play: How Claude Shannon Invented the Information Age* (New York, 2017), pp. 38–41.

quantities is only limited by the number and exhaustiveness of its resources, all of which had to be known and tabulated in advance. Fortunately, under Harvey Fletcher Bell Labs had already devoted much of the previous decade to quantifying the parameters of human and mechanical audition in pursuit of improved transmission and reproduction of speech and music. Applied to population figures, the new art of statistical analysis could only progress in the presence of a similarly exhaustive database of personal characteristics, any combination of which might comprise a definition or sufficient description of an individual subject. Novelist Robert Musil's title *The Man without Qualities* (*Der Mann ohne Eigenschaften*, 1940–3) addresses the paradoxical consequences of statistical anonymity, an image of human destiny embraced by the Mass Observation movement of the 1930s, and expressed in iconic imagery by prominent surrealists, including René Magritte's faceless man in a bowler hat. A similar conception of the faceless consumer underwrites the techniques and tactics of online marketing in today's smartphone era.

At Princeton, Shannon consulted Hermann Weyl on the mathematics of noise reduction and signal compression issues in telecommunications. Noise was the bane of the telecommunications industry. In the past, the industry had dealt with noise on the line by limiting the transmission bandwidth to frequencies in the mid-range, gravely reducing signal definition. The vocoder had been developed to thread the outline of a speech signal through the needle's eye of a cable system designed in the previous century for Morse code messages. Now the proposal was to add noise to voice transmission as a cloak of invisibility. Suppose, Shannon wondered, if noise were treated mathematically, not as the problem, but as part of the answer? On the basis of his recent experience in statistical analysis, Shannon knew that uncertainty could be quantified, and the same formulae previously used to address noise reduction and interpret population statistics could also be applied to the probability of winning at poker, or even voice or text messaging.

Weyl was intrigued, but sceptical. A former colleague of Albert Einstein at Zürich, he had succeeded David Hilbert to the chair of mathematics at Göttingen University in 1932, only to be offered a position at Princeton to escape persecution by the Nazi regime, an offer finally taken up in October 1933. A specialist in the dynamics of explosions and valued authority in the emerging field of atomic energy, Weyl's formulations relating to radio wave propagation had already attracted the attention of the telecommunications industry.[12] Nestling in pages of mathematical formulae, Weyl's grand vision of cosmic harmony, laid bare in

[12] Charles R. Burrows, 'Existence of a Surface Wave in Radio Propagation'. *Nature* 138 (1936), p. 284.

the influential *Space, Time, and Matter* (1922), had become essential background reading for the composer of *L'Astronome*, an apocalyptic scenario inspired by the prophecies of Nikola Tesla, and yet another project for which Varèse earnestly sought audio industry approval and investment.[13]

Shannon agonized over the mathematics of continuity, teaching himself to juggle while balancing on a unicycle, an act of conscious mastery of the intuitive human ability to offset a tendency to fall sideways by moving forward, and vice versa, in actions reproducing the normal function of an animal inner ear. Probability theory on its own could not account for an animal's ability to pounce, or an infant's ability to reach for an object, let alone deduce the future path of a moving object in the field of vision. Tantalisingly, Potter's team had already succeeded in identifying a theme or Ariadne's thread in continuous speech, in the form of resonance bar 2, the most mobile and connected of the three principal formant regions of visible speech.[14]

Shannon hoped Weyl might assist in establishing a connection between the pattern of fluctuation in the external parameters of the speaking voice and determination of the flow of intelligence mediated by speech. As a specialist in radiant energy – all forms of which postulate continuities of space, time, and motion – Weyl was no doubt preoccupied in 1942 with calculations relating to the controlled detonation of an atomic bomb within a carefully designed capsule, a proposition leaving unresolved the bigger question of how the total energy released by the ensuing explosion would propagate through, over, and beyond the earth's surface. In the nineteenth century it had been customary for scholars of fluid dynamics to ignore the contributions of friction, turbulence, and internal cancellations in their equations as unquantifiable variables involving unwanted infinities. The modern world of telecommunications made no such allowances. The real world was invincibly impure, noisy, and unpredictable. Nor, in the previous half century, had the science of architectural acoustics succeeded in determining appropriate formulae even for the dissemination of musical energy in the safe, placid environment of a concert hall, arguing that the calculation of delayed reflections remained invincibly complex. Weyl's *Gruppentheorie* (1931) would re-emerge in the mid-1950s as a referential basis for Stockhausen's *Gruppen* for three orchestras, an advance on the pointillist aesthetic of the composer's *Punkte* and Boulez's *Polyphonie X*, not to mention *Mode de valeurs* by Messiaen and Cage's *Music of Changes*.

The failure of current mathematical theory to address continuous energy propagation took its toll. Eventually the musician in Shannon – an amateur

---

13 'Cosmic Noise'. Artem Saakian, *Radio Wave Propagation Fundamentals* (Boston, MA, 2011), pp. 332–3.

14 Potter, Kopp, and Kopp, *Visible Speech*, p. 308.

jazz clarinet player – sought an alternative approach. Since a continuous sequence of inflected hand gestures in an electrostatic field generated by an upright radio wave antenna enabled the theremin player to produce a modulated voicelike melody, in theory such a movement could be defined mathematically in the same terms as a quasi-random path in a spacelike field. In following the melody produced by the movement of a violinist's finger up and down the string, an observer was calculating where the melody was likely to go next on the basis of its previous history, and knowing the limits to which the finger might stray.

To describe the path of a melody as a 'random walk', or more graphically, as 'a drunk man going for a walk', is a convenient, if misleading, metaphor, since it is neither the melody nor the player but rather the listener who is unable to figure out where it is going next. At heart, the mystery hiding within the random walk analogy is the groove of a gramophone recording, a path which the stylus is obliged to follow insensibly, but one giving rise to a signal the ear instantly recognizes as intentional music or speech.

> It may seem curious that it was a Bell Telephone Laboratories Group which came forward with new ideas and techniques to apply to the [anti-aircraft aiming] problems. . . . There are surprisingly close and valid analogies between the fire control prediction problem and certain basic problems in communications engineering. . . . Both problems demanded the quick calculation of probabilities – the probable structure of a message, or the probable location of the target at any given moment – both required high-level statistical inference.[15]

In 1948, Shannon published 'A Mathematical Theory of Communication' in two parts. Reviewed online, the text, while difficult to follow, is of interest to historians of music because of its impact on a small number of influential composers and theorists in the second half of the twentieth century, and the curious symbiosis that arose between composers and information science during and after the Cold War era. The production of music does not figure in Shannon's original document. But the processes summarized below were destined to inspire further attempts to 'compose' melodies in a particular idiom or style.

> In telegraphy, for example, messages consist of sequences of letters grouped in words and separated by blanks. Such sequences are not completely random. In general, they form sentences and have the statistical structure of, say, English. . . . A physical system, or a mathematical model of a system which produces . . . a sequence of symbols governed by a set of probabilities, is

[15] Soni and Goodman, *A Mind at Play*, p. 86.

> known as a stochastic process. . . . Any stochastic process which produces a discrete sequence of symbols chosen from a finite set may be considered a discrete source. . . . [A discrete source] will include such cases as:
>
> 1. Natural written languages such as English, German, Chinese.
> 2. Continuous information sources that have been rendered discrete by some quantizing process.
> 3. Mathematical cases where we merely define abstractly a stochastic process which generates a sequence of symbols.[16]

Case 3 above gives rise to subgroups A, B, C, D, and E of randomly generated letter sequences representing increasingly sophisticated selection protocols. In C, for example, the probability of a letter being chosen depends on the letter immediately preceding. In D, sequences of letters may be elevated to the status of 'words', each word itself a unit of meaning with an associated degree of probability.

Under a heading 'The Series of Approximations to English' Shannon's paper reviews a progression of six degrees of stochastic ('targeted') selection of letter combinations or groups of increasing comprehensibility. In the most basic, zero-order approximation, characters are selected at random from an alphabet of twenty-six letters and a space, without conditions.

> XFOML RXKHRJFFJUJ ZLPWCFWKCYJ FFJEYVKCQSGHYD
> QPAAMKLBZAACIBZLHJQD.

In the above randomly generated string of 62 characters, no T and no N appear, two of the most statistically frequent letters in English prose. A first-order approximation is weighted to conform with the statistical distribution of letters in English. In the example provided, for instance, the weighted distribution is almost too perfect:

> OCRO HLI RGWR NMIELWIS EU LL NBNESEBYA TH EEI
> ALHENHTTPA
> OOBTTVA NAH BRL.

Second-order approximation requires each following letter or blank space to be selected by a look-up process in which the experimenter randomly opens an English-language text, looks for a word containing the previous letter, then writes down the letter following. The resulting interlinked two-letter groups or *digrams* are authentically English, given that every pairing, though random, is a provable two-letter combination in the English language.

[16] Claude Shannon, 'A Mathematical Theory of Communication' – Harvard Math Department, math.harvard.edu, 4 September 2018.

> ON IE ANTSOUTINYS ARE T INCTORE ST BE S DEAMY ACHIN D ILONASIVE TUCOOWE AT TEAQSONARE FUSO TIZIN ANDY TOBE SEACE CTISBE.

The above second-order sequence is credited by Shannon with generating recognizable parts of five or six English words, presumably including *achin* [machine], *lo**sive [explosive], *ea*sona*e [reasonable, resonate], fus* [fuse], *outin* [routine], and t*nct*re [tincture], terms implying the use of a dictionary of chemistry as a look-up text.

For a higher, third-order (trigram) approximation, the look-up process searches the data source for pre-selected two-letter combinations, and records the letter (or space) that follows:

> IN NO IST LAT WHEY CRATICT FROURE BIRS PONDENOME OF DEMONSTURES OF THE REPTAGIN IS REGOACTIONA OF CRE.

Stand-out groups in the above third-order collection are denom[ination], or *enome [genome], demonst*r**es [demonstrates], re**action, [demo]cratic.

For higher levels, the selection process moves – somewhat arbitrarily, perhaps – from groups of three letters to whole words. In first-order *word* approximation, Shannon observes, 'words are chosen independently but with their appropriate frequencies'. What that means is unclear. Either Shannon has access to a register of words in the English language classified by frequency of use – for example, Ogden's *Basic English* (1930) comes to mind – or the author is continuing to select words from a randomly chosen book on the assumption that the distribution of words in any given English language text will conform sufficiently to their normal statistical distribution in the language at large.

> REPRESENTING AND SPEEDILY IS AN GOOD APT OR COME CAN DIFFERENT NATURAL HERE HE THE A IN CAME THE TO OF TO EXPERT GRAY COME TO FURNISHES THE LINE MESSAGE HAD BE THESE.

Ultimately, in second-order word approximation, 'the word transition probabilities are correct but no further structure is included' – meaning, a following word is chosen according to its appearance in a randomly chosen source text containing the previous word.

> THE HEAD AND IN FRONTAL ATTACK ON AN ENGLISH WRITER THAT THE CHARACTER OF THIS POINT IS THEREFORE ANOTHER METHOD FOR THE LETTERS THAT THE TIME OF WHO EVER TOLD THE PROBLEM FOR AN UNEXPECTED.

In substance and style, the above reads like a cut-up article from a newspaper. Shannon concludes, 'the resemblance to ordinary English text increases quite noticeably at each of the above steps. Note that these [latest] samples have reasonably good structure out to about twice the range that is taken into account in their construction'.

Stockhausen recalled similar class exercises in Information Theory with Werner Meyer-Eppler in 1954 and 1955:

> [Meyer-Eppler] was engaged in studying statistics, because he wanted to know more precisely what all the different sounds were, and analyzing the wave structure of noises and consonants in language led him to statistical methods of description and analysis. He would give us exercises demonstrating the principles of the Markoff series; in one we were given cut-outs of individual letters from newspaper articles, and we had to put them in sequence by a chance operation and see what sort of a text came out.[17]

At first glance, Shannon is addressing the ambitious task of 'growing' meaningful word strings in English (or any given language) by a mechanical matching process which over time becomes increasingly reliable statistically. One begins by generating clouds of letters as bait to attract second, third, and more letters as they are found to occur in actual words in the chosen language. Essentially the exercise aims to arrive at a statistical description of the target language by random selection within the language itself, which is treated as a database.

Shannon's upgrade of the selection process from letters to whole words in sequence can be seen to correspond to software engines of today that trawl the internet for keywords to trigger negative messages in response. Shannon himself set the process in motion by composing an unpublished but prescient article in 1949 about a fictitious evil scientist inventing a machine capable of 'randomly stitching together agitprop phrases in a way that approximates human language . . . to produce an endless flood of demoralizing statements'.[18]

Shannon's groundbreaking paper was published the same year as Boulez's essay 'Incidences actuelles de Berg', in which the composer Alban Berg is castigated for his habit of incorporating illustrative elements in his musical fabric: ciphers, and even recognizable words and phrases – notably J.S. Bach's chorale 'Es ist genug', which appears like magic out of the twelve-tone matrix of Berg's 1935 Violin Concerto. Boulez's manifest irritation at the outwardly spontaneous (albeit carefully crafted) emergence of a tonal and historical melody from the rigid confines of the series is offset by his admiration for the

---

[17] Karlheinz Stockhausen, *Stockhausen on Music* (London, 1989), pp. 43–62.

[18] Soni and Goodman, *A Mind at Play*, pp. 148, 149n.

manner in which Berg derives multiple themes – representing contrasting personalities – from the series on which the opera *Lulu* is composed. Such opinions on Boulez's part are consistent with twelve-tone music becoming a suitable candidate for cryptanalysis in the 1930s, only to be overtaken in 1949 at Messiaen's behest by a system of more obviously dissociated serial orders and rotations.

During the course of his exposition, Shannon's defence of a selection procedure using a randomly chosen initial letter or word as a prompt to initiate a search within a data file for a following letter or word *consistent* with the combination's normal frequency of occurrence within the target language is observed spontaneously to mutate into a logical claim that the initial letter or word *influences* the following, randomly selected letter or word, seemingly in an attempt to camouflage the plain reality that pattern recognition based on actual text material is invariably subject to the internal distributions and sequencing habits of the source language or text. Having begun his career as a specialist in analogue computation applied to aiming mechanisms for use in defence artillery, subsequently drafted into devising a sorting mechanism for the analysis of population statistics, then reapplied to an encryption programme involving the structured disintegration of an analogue signal (the speaking voice), Shannon ends by proposing a model for reconstructing encrypted text messages by an improbably wasteful method of digital guesswork reliant on being executed by computer at electric speed. In the battle between competing forces of digital (Morse code) and analogue (speech), however, speed would prevail.

The British were into high fidelity, improving the quality of analogue signalling, but their American collaborators were more interested in developing selection mechanisms for winning at roulette and poker. In consulting Weyl, Shannon had sought help in preserving the integrity of the continuum; but Weyl could not help him, and Shannon ended by surrendering to the forces of statistical association. The juggling poet of unicycling was reborn as the guru of the Monte Carlo method and defender of a world view that says life is a gamble, you have to make the best of the hand you are dealt, the object is to win by second-guessing your opponents, and winning is profit.

RCA and ILLIAC Synthesizers

Harry Olson (1901–82) was head of acoustical research at the Radio Corporation of America from 1935 until his retirement in 1967. Early in his career as a microphone and loudspeaker specialist, he developed the RCA 44 and 77 ribbon microphones, instruments of a bidirectional or 'figure of eight' design selectively responsive to sound sources directly in front or behind the plane of the ribbon, and insensitive to sounds incident from either side. Olson also developed long-throw speakers for public address and movie theatre applications, again with the aim of controlling the direction of sound inside an auditorium and minimizing the effects of internal reflection. In 1942, when the United States entered the war, he was assigned to work on the development of an undersea microphone for submarine detection. His wide-ranging research portfolio, which included a 1950 patent related to the management of concert hall acoustics, reflected the changing communications objectives of the US military and the audio industry's priorities in acoustical design, expressed in a high-definition, flat-plane aesthetic optimized for radio reception and relatively indifferent to spatial realism. The search for optimal definition in recorded music encouraged a layered, mosaic approach to audio imaging, freely employing cosmetic technical strategies to counter the distorting effects of compressing a broadband signal into the limited bandwidths of radio and telephone of the period. In an archive IEEE interview Olson recalled that the original decision to limit the operational bandwidth of domestic AM radio and phono playback equipment to an upper threshold of 5,000 Hertz had been taken mainly in order to eliminate transmission noise, an expedient subsequently defended by the industry on economic grounds, to optimize the number of channels available for business.[19]

The Olson-Belar synthesizer[20] created with Herbert Belar (1901–97) was the offspring of an idea that had been circulating within RCA under David Sarnoff's leadership since the 1930s. In those times the commercial objectives of a music synthesizer were artistically trivial but commercially significant, aiming at automating the production and assembly of advertising jingles, incidental music cues for movies and radio, and sound effects. It was an idea of its time; during the Great Depression the costs associated with producing musical clips and inserts, music of negligible artistic value, still involved hiring composers and musicians, booking studio time, and meeting copyright liabilities, all of which represented a significant financial burden to the radio and movie industries. The concept and design of a synthesizer took shape around a credible and potentially substantial niche market for non-copyright musical cues, a role previously assigned to music-hall bands and movie accompanists, reflecting a perception of music as decorative incident that persists into the twenty-first century.

[19] Harry F. Olson, 'An Interview conducted by Mark Heyer, 14 July 1975', https://ethw.org, 21 September 2018.

[20] Harry F. Olson, *Music, Physics, and Engineering* (New York, 1967), pp. 441–8.

During the war, extended range recording was developed, a process hastened because the standard AM bandwidth of 150–3,500 Hertz was demonstrably insufficient for training in aircraft identification by ear, or voice recognition for telephone surveillance. After the war, despite the introduction of newly branded 'high fidelity' microphones and recording media, including the launch by Columbia in 1948 of the silent surface extended play vinyl disc, the record industry continued to resist a move to stereo for the best part of a further decade. In addition to the cost implications of two-channel reproduction, the introduction of stereo implied a return to hearing music performed in its natural surroundings and in realistic balance. (Ironically, in marketing a superior recording medium and lightweight tracking system valued for largely eliminating surface noise, the audio industry created a new and paradoxical association of technical excellence with absence of surface noise, a quality feature to be exploited by John Cage in his 1952 silent composition, lasting the four-and-a-half-minute duration of a single side of a pre-war 78 rpm shellac disc.)

Olson was involved in experiments conducted by RCA to determine whether audiences were ready to accept high-fidelity radio and recorded music in place of the rounded tones of AM radio and associated rolloff of frequencies above 5,000 Hertz. Including the development of adjustable acoustic screens to limit or pass high frequencies, Olson's test regime would contribute to the development of programmable acoustic panels eventually installed in the Salle de Projection at Boulez's IRCAM.

Sarnoff saw no merit in having to pay copyright dues on single-use background music items of a few seconds' duration, no doubt considering that the role of a movie accompanist or hotel lobby pianist could in principle be filled by more or less random selection from a limited register of musical types pre-classified by character, temperament, melody, rhythm, texture, harmony, instrumental colour, and tempo. In endorsing a prevailing view within the entertainment industry of the role of music as spontaneously improvised incidental content drawing on a database of collective memory to reflect the emotional demands of a visual script, Sarnoff is an important link between John Cage, information scientist John von Neumann, and Claude Shannon.

Sarnoff's perception of recorded music in the 1930s as a virtual art of interior decoration of a prearranged architecture – movie, production line, or radio play – is consistent both with John Cage's composing strategy of the 1930s represented by a strictly timed assembly line of scenes combined with improvised content, and with Messiaen's development during the same period of a theory of music defined as a ritually decorative, quasi-improvisatory art. In their different ways, Cage and Sarnoff were pursuing the identical goal of a functional music to be created 'without apparent intention': Cage for reasons attributed somewhat disingenuously to Eastern philosophy, Sarnoff for reasons of hard-nosed commercial expediency and in order to cement a culture of anonymity within the music profession – at least in Hollywood, if not on Broadway.

From 1952 to 1954 Olson collaborated with Herbert Belar in designing and assembling the wall-to-wall suite of devices collectively comprising the RCA Electronic Music Synthesizer. A former student of Carl E. Seashore at Iowa University in the 1920s, Olson was guided by personal recollection of Seashore's wish for 'an instrument that could produce any musical tone, regardless of whether it had ever been produced or not'. Seashore's own publications in music cognition and performance had relied on photographic evidence of accuracy of intonation and comparing measurements of reproducing piano roll timings with the published score.

Purely on its own terms, Sarnoff's synthesizer concept resembled a vending automat or jukebox on which stored items could be dialled up and played back in sequence. Items of music or sound effects could be selected from a subset of disc recorded sounds, cued up in sequence, and played as recorded, following the practice of 'grams' music and sound effects operators in radio drama productions. A separate use envisioned for the music synthesizer, Olson wrote, was the production of background music for hire in the form of piped entertainment or gramophone records. Mothballed during the war, revived as a prototype in the 1950s, by the time of its official launch in 1955 the Mark I model, incorporating an acetate disc recorder as printout, was arguably already obsolete.

Sarnoff's cost-saving goals from the 1930s included the production for hire of synthesized cover versions of non-copyright songs to be used as mood-enhancing background music in factories and supermarkets without payment of performer royalties. Trial recordings from 1952 employing the Mark I Synthesizer are preserved online, including arrangements from the silent movie era of 'Blue Skies' by Irving Berlin 'in the style of a dance band', and 'Nola' by Felix Arndt, described as 'arranged in the style of the piano'. A 'Stephen Foster Medley' dated December 1952 showcased the synthesizer's versatility at imitating 'bowed, plucked, and struck instruments; air, mechanical, and lip reed instruments; and percussion instruments'.

By 1952, the long-awaited arrival of extended range high-fidelity vinyl recording had created new markets for exotic and early music employing historic and ethnic instruments, entire collections of which were underwritten by institutions such as UNESCO, the Smithsonian Museum, Deutsche Grammophon's Archiv division, and similar organizations. During the 1950s, Olson worked on the design of a 200-syllable 'Phonetic Typewriter', a voice-operated Dictaphone intended to print out memoranda from voice dictation in a version of phonetic spelling. American interest in syllabic word assembly of this kind coincided with Boulez's composition of *Le marteau sans maître* and Stockhausen's electronic *Gesang der Jünglinge*. Olson's patented 'voiced sound fundamental frequency detector', launched in 1968, was designed as a self-adjusting filter for artificial speech, to follow the accented timing of a speaking or singing voice while simultaneously adjusting the formant structures of associated syllables – a prototype envelope follower, in other words, of the kind adopted by Boulez to allow an artificial intelligence to follow the timing cues of a solo player in works such as *Répons* and *Anthèmes II*.[21]

Optical templates based on vocoder samples, launched in 1954 for artificial speaking devices, inspired the block graphics of Stockhausen's score of *Electronic Study II*, and in 1959 the radical notations of *Refrain*, *Zyklus*, and original concept of *Momente* as a mutable score with optional transparent overlays. The use of printed transparent sheets as templates for optical tone production had been proposed experimentally during the 1930s, in Russia and elsewhere, as a means of improving the audio quality of movie soundtracks. Percy Grainger and John Cage were among composers experimenting in the 1950s with hand-drawn notations on transparent sheets intended for translation into sound by optical reading devices. The use of a graphics interface for optical sound generation on which a composer could improvise freely aroused enthusiasm among a few professionals, including Daphne Oram in Britain, and inspired a naïve but eager younger generation of Darmstadt graphics experimenters, despite the quality of both optical sound and graphics scores being rejected by audio professionals as incoherent, irrational, coarse in quality, labour-intensive, out of control, and subject to contamination by unwanted noise.

While conforming retroactively to the aesthetic and commercial priorities of an older generation, the design and performance requirements of Olson and Belar's RCA Mark I and Mark II instruments were ill-adapted to meet post-war commercial needs and realities. By 1955, the movie world had expanded into widescreen, and as Sarnoff's hopes of profiting from automation were rapidly diminishing, the development costs of the RCA Synthesizers were eclipsing any profit to be anticipated from replacing human musical expertise by machine.

Among academics, Shannon's 'Mathematical Theory of Communication' attracted the attention of William Weaver and Louis Ridenour at the University of Illinois, along with an eager constituency of playful engineers with access to computers. A joint investigation by computer programmer Leonard M. Isaacson and Lejaren A. Hiller, a chemistry professor at the

[21] Harry F. Olson and Herbert Belar, 'Voiced Sound Fundamental Frequency Detector', Patent no. US3400215A (1968).

University of Illinois, sought to apply Shannon's information protocols to the spontaneous generation of a music that might ultimately pass muster as serious art. Their initiative involved developing

> a process and technique ... for writing [composing] music by means of a digital computer. In this process random integers, considered to be equivalent to musical notes, are first generated and then selected and screened by mathematical operations which express the rules of musical composition. ... The composition ... employs the Monte Carlo method and therefore operates on the laws of chance or ... random probability.[22]

The ILLIAC computer on which Hiller and Isaacson worked was a copy of a military machine originally designed to compute ballistics trajectories, an instrument to which the collaborators had been assigned to solve problems relating to the production of complex polymer chains for the manufacture of synthetic rubber. Hiller had studied composition with Milton Babbitt, who encouraged him to apply Shannon's mathematical strategies to music composition. The production of chains of molecules is an investigation of rules of chemical connection, and in that sense potentially similar to generating melodies by identifying the laws and valencies of interval attraction. More prosaically, adapting the formulae governing the formation of chain molecules to produce the equivalent in strings of notes had the potential to lead to a fast and efficient method of assessing by ear the viability of chemical rules of association. Among Hiller and Isaacson's better-known compositions, the *Illiac Suite for String Quartet* (1955–7) consists of a sequence of short movements representing a *Gradus ad Parnassum* of probabilistic exercises informed by rules of harmony applicable in successive periods of Western classical music from diatonic harmony in the style of J.S. Bach to chromatic, atonal, and twelve-tone styles in the twentieth century.

In another experiment, the melody note collections of eleven popular songs by Stephen Foster were transposed into the same key of D major and shuffled together, yielding a collective pitch distribution curve of twelve notes extending over an octave and fourth, B3–E5. Based on the weighted distributions of notes in this collection, new melodies were generated in conformity with Shannon's first-order selection probability, to see if any resembled Stephen Foster songs. A second-order selection process was based on the relative frequency of two-note combinations; finally a third-order approximation looked for three-note groups. At the end of their inquiries, the investigators optimistically concluded that

[22] Lejaren A. Hiller and Leonard M. Isaacson, *Experimental Music: Composition with an Electronic Computer* (New York, 1959).

> There is considerable redundancy, and as a consequence, a definite pattern in the music of Stephen Foster. These results indicate that a composing machine employing a random probability system may be developed, which will produce music which will sound like Stephen Foster songs but will be new. . . . The electronic music composing machine will be of value to the composer in the production of new music of [this] type.[23]

Some years later, a non-random fluctuation in nature was adopted by Charles Dodge to provide the melodic contour of *Earth's Magnetic Field*, the composer employing an IBM 360 model 91 at Columbia University to assign numerical values to a sample pattern of Kp (global geomagnetic activity) indices for the time period 1 January–6 February 1961. The resulting interval sequence was subsequently adjusted at Bell Labs to conform with optional diatonic or chromatic scales.

'Computational composition in the United States got its start,' observed Matthew Guerrieri in a recent article, 'quite literally, in the off-hour downtime of the military-industrial complex.'[24] At ElectroData, a Pasadena firm acquired by Burroughs, the adding-machine manufacturer, a Datatron computer was programmed by engineers Martin L. Klein and Douglas Bolitho to compose melodies in a popular idiom, the authors admitting with refreshing candour, 'We set out to prove that if human beings could write "popular music" of poor quality at the rate of a song an hour, we could write it just as bad with a computing machine, but faster.' The article continued:

> Klein and Bolitho searched among the top one hundred pop songs of the year, looking for patterns. They came up with three principal rules:
>
> 1. There are between 35 and 60 different [discrete] notes in a popular song.
> 2. A popular song has the following pattern: part A, which runs 8 measures and contains about 18 to 25 notes; part A, repeated; part B, which contains 8 measures and between 17 and 35 notes; part A, again repeated.
> 3. If five notes move successively in an upward direction, the sixth note is downward and vice versa.[25]

The Datatron computer was employed by the US military, among other tasks, 'to calculate simulated dispersal patterns for airborne chemical and biological

[23] Olson, *Music, Physics, and Engineering*, p. 434.

[24] Matthew Guerrieri, 'Automation Divine: Early Computer Music and the Selling of the Cold War'. *NewMusicBox* (10 October 2018), https://newmusicusa.org.

[25] Martin L. Klein, 'Syncopation by Automation'. *Radio Electronics* vol. XXVIII, no. 6 (1957), pp. 36–8.

weapons' – propagation of energy calculations of the kind to which Hermann Weyl had devoted much of his professional career.[26]

In *The Naked Lunch*, an experimental novel co-written with Brion Gysin, writer William S. Burroughs, grandson of the founder of the Burroughs firm, employed randomization techniques inspired by the surrealist poet Tristan Tzara and referenced in *Theory of Games and Economic Behavior* (1944), a pioneer text in Game Theory by John von Neumann and Oskar Morgenstern.

> All writing is in fact cut-ups. Cutting and rearranging a page of written words introduces a new dimension. . . . This is where Rimbaud was going with his color of vowels. . . . Dr Neumann in his *Theory of Games and Economic Behavior* introduces the cut-up method of random action into game and military strategy. . . . If your strategy is at some point determined . . . by [some] random factor your opponent will gain no advantage from knowing your strategy since he cannot predict the move. The cut-up method could be used to advantage in processing scientific data.[27]

In a further series of experiments modelled on the graded complexity of operations outlined in Shannon's 1948 paper, Hiller and Isaacson generated a string of random numbers and then sought by various means to scale the resulting interval pattern to render the number sequence as an intelligible melody, initially confined to a seven-note C major diatonic scale, extended with duplications over a two-octave range; then revised to conform to a statistically weighted diatonic idiom based on the songs of Stephen Foster, with added rules of association; and finally to the chromatic scale. Each choice of scale and accompanying rules acted as a kind of filter to influence the occurrence of consonant intervals and sequences in the style of Foster. In restricting options to the scale of C major, an acceptable result would be most likely to occur; an agreeable quality was less likely if the same formulae were applied to a chromatic scale, in which the element of dissonance or harmonic ambiguity is more broadly distributed. More complicated applications of theory ranged from zero-order harmonic [interval] probability to the calculation of weighted distributions of intervals in varying degrees.[28] Hiller and Isaacson's 'Table of Functions for the generation of Markoff-Chain music' invites comparison with the table of graded degrees of dissonance of intervals within the octave provided in Paul Hindemith's *The Craft of Musical Composition*. In turn, Hindemith appears to have based his dissonance classifications on

[26] Guerrieri, 'Automation Divine'.

[27] William Burroughs, 'The Cut-up Method of Brion Gysin'. In John Calder ed., *A William Burroughs Reader* (London, 1982), pp. 268–78.

[28] Olson, *Music, Physics, and Engineering*, p. 444.

a combination of personal intuition and historical classifications of interval ratios by Euler and Max Planck.[29]

A Computer Cantata (1963) devised by Lejaren Hiller and Robert Baker was designed to test a package of compositional procedures titled MUSICOMP devised for use with an IBM 7090 computer. The MUSICOMP package was programmed to select and assemble figures of musical speech into simple verse and refrain formations derived from harmony textbooks: a second device, the CSX-1 computer, acting as interface between the synthesized score instructions and a selection of electronic tone and noise generators. In addition to composing music, MUSICOMP also composed the words, producing texts ranging stochastically by degrees from randomly selected phonemes resembling the speech of a fictional alien civilization, through to English.

> The texts ... are five stochastic approximations to spoken English derived from a synthesis by a computer of stochastic phoneme sequences ... prepared with the ILLIAC, the original Illinois University electronic digital computer [and] based on the statistical analysis of a corpus of English text drawn at random from the publication *PLAYS, The Drama Magazine for Young People*. ... Zeroth through fourth-order transition frequencies for the phonemic structure of this material were computed. ... [They include the following] example for *Strophe I* (Zeroth-order Approximation) approximately rendered as: '*sh*hlkâchg # # ml*th*älnôê # ëûdåôâ*sh*îsnî # îô*zh*mpäthy etc.'

– 'for which a pronunciation key is given to help the vocalist', the author helpfully adds.[30]

In 1967 John Cage took up a position as composer in residence at Illinois University. Five years previously Cage had been requested by harpsichordist Antoinette Vischer to compose a work for her instrument, and on assuming the residency Cage asked Lejaren Hiller to assist. The result was *HPSCHD*, a simultaneous event for a trio of baroque, modern, and electronic harpsichords accompanied by up to fifty-one tapes of melodies synthesized by the ILLIAC II computer in equal-tempered scales ranging from a mathematically exact (that is, tonally skewed) pentatonic mode to a microtonal 56-division octave worthy of Mexican composer Julián Carrillo. Cage had no computer programming skills, nor was he particularly fond of the harpsichord as a sonority – who knows why? Possibly because the instrument is emblematic of the baroque era, an association with the early music movement the composer was anxious to avoid; or perhaps because the instrument sounded uncomfortably similar to the prepared

[29] Peter Pesic, *Music and the Making of Modern Science* (Cambridge, MA, 2014), pp. 255–67.
[30] Peter Yates, *Twentieth Century Music* (London, 1967), pp. 319–20.

piano. Hiller suggested they take the *Musical Dice Game* (Musikalisches Würfelspiel, K.294d), attributed to Mozart, as a point of departure.

HPSCHD (its six-character title reflecting the programming conventions of the time) is best discussed without reference to aesthetics – or rather, from a perspective representing the preferences of Information Theory. In many ways, the harpsichord is actually an interesting choice. First, it is by design a highly intellectual digital instrument engineered to deliver a totally even touch, thus a medium without accent or expression. Second, its plucking action releases a sharp tone of rapid decay, meaning that fast or slow notes sound identical, like a musical box. This has the interesting consequence that a variation in tempo is perceived as a variation in density of notes. Third, these same characteristics are typical of computer-generated sounds of the early 1960s. Indeed, harpsichord tonal imagery is similar to computer-generated sound of the period to a point where one has to ask, are the two instruments conceptually related? Is Bach possibly using the harpsichord to study pattern formation and compute note relations in analogous fashion to a mathematician manipulating number relations on a digital computer in 1967?

Perhaps to avoid potentially embarrassing comparisons, the selection of Mozart's Musical Dice Game as a basis of invention diverts attention from Bach to Mozart. According to biographer James Bohn, 'Cage had noticed that melodies of J.S. Bach exhibited consistently diatonic scalar movement, whereas Mozart's tended to wander into chromatic and chord-related note sequences evolving in the direction of greater complexity' – an observation in interesting contradiction of the law of increasing entropy.[31] In reality, Mozart's composing style is indelibly associated with the fortepiano, the Italian hammer-action successor to the harpsichord, an instrument combining infinite volatility of accent with tone and amplitude variation, gestural power, and controllable sustain.

Assigning Mozart to the harpsichord – even an electronic version of the instrument – was anachronistic even in 1967. In other respects, however, *HPSCHD* addressed topics of interest to information science. These included: (1) Simultaneous transmissions of music representing multiple channels of an information medium; (2) A majority of channels by the same composer, representing a preponderance of musical data strings statistically consistent with one another according to a distribution of probabilities still to be determined; (3) Computer-generated Mozart-related tone sequences expressing degrees of virtual frequency shifting, or scales of interval expansion and compression; (4)

[31] James Bohn, 'Lejaren Hiller: Early Experiments in Computer and Electronic Music'. In Lillian Hoddeson ed., *No Boundaries: University of Illinois Vignettes* (Champaign, IL, 2004), pp. 293–303.

Options allowing for the incorporation (for comparison or concealment) of items by Mozart or later composers, including Hiller and Cage, irrespective of whether they were composed for harpsichord. Hence, taking the long view, *HPSCHD* is an informal inquiry into the statistics of Mozart's musical speech as a probabilistic distribution of notes, runs, and figures; at the same time, the accompanying computer-generated tapes allow Mozart's personal brand of chromaticism to be audited in continuous comparison with alternative scales and degrees of expansion or compression, as if processed for transmission by cable or alternative media of limited bandwidth.[32]

Requested by a friendly editor to contribute an article explaining in simple language what modern music is for and its relationship to the listener, Milton Babbitt's account of modern composition as an intellectual enterprise preferably conducted in secret under laboratory conditions, laid bare in a tell-all article unfortunately titled 'Who cares if you listen?' and published in 1958, sought instead to perpetuate a culture of secrecy and exclusiveness prevailing in advanced musical research in the United States from the late 1920s.[33] The same Cold War tactic of benign evasion would be adopted by Boulez and Cage in conversations with the music press.

Babbitt's musical tastes were formed by a combination of early training as a songwriter, jazz player and arranger, formal university studies of Schoenberg's twelve-tone music, and war service as a mathematics instructor and researcher at Princeton University in the mid-1940s. For the remainder of a long and influential academic career Babbitt refused to discuss his wartime research, though it requires little imagination for a reader to infer from the list of his publications and musical interests that the application of set theory to musical analysis in subject areas of interest to communications intelligence played a key role. Presumably for want of suitably qualified assessors, but possibly for security reasons, Babbitt's doctoral dissertation 'The Function of Set Structure in the Twelve-Tone System', submitted after completion of his war service, was declined consideration by Columbia University. Babbitt's research considered the structural implications of Schoenberg's twelve-tone method, as a guide to parsing the identity relations of the composer's musical language. The difficulty of Babbitt's task is explained in part as a consequence of Schoenberg's own reluctance to cooperate with or endorse technical studies he regarded as of merely secondary interest. During this time Schoenberg's refusal to abandon traditional gestures and forms of musical rhetoric emerged as a source of grievance to a younger generation including Messiaen, Boulez, and

[32] James Pritchett, *The Music of John Cage* (Cambridge, 1993), pp. 159–61.

[33] Milton Babbitt, 'Who Cares if You Listen?' (1958). In Elliott Schwartz and Barney Childs eds., *Contemporary Composers on Contemporary Music* (New York, 1967), pp. 243–50.

Stockhausen, and was cited as part justification for Boulez's ostentatious dismissal of Schoenberg's relevance following the latter's death in 1951.

By 1958, when Babbitt's 'Who Cares If You Listen?' article appeared, the analogue RCA Mark II Synthesizer, still awaiting installation at the Columbia-Princeton Center, was practically obsolete. Hopes remained high that an upgraded Mark II version, purchased at enormous expense in 1959 and incorporating modest improvements including a tape recorder and microphone input, might become more than just the expensive centrepiece of a prestige composing and research facility run jointly by Columbia and Princeton Universities. In less than a decade the Mark II behemoth was rapidly being superseded by a new generation of voltage-controlled analogue tone synthesizers, the latter soon to be challenged by the arrival of digital music computation and synthesis simulation software developed by Max Mathews and others at Bell Labs from the same stochastic model of music computation inspired by Claude Shannon's Information Theory and initially implemented by Lejaren Hiller and Leonard Isaacson on the University of Illinois's ILLIAC I digital computer.

Max Mathews had originally applied to join the Audio Research Department at Bell Labs to study new and better ways of compressing and encoding speech so it could be transmitted over the very limited capacity wires and radio bandwidths available in 1954.[34] Immediately following his arrival at Bell Labs, with the blessing of John R. Pierce, Mathews was assigned to work on the development of a prototype digital system called GROOVE to incorporate MUSIC composing software, tone generation, stochastic composition by numbers, and instrument simulation.

2 Stockhausen's *Helicopter String Quartet*

The *Helicopter String Quartet* is a Stockhausen composition dating from 1993 in which members of a string quartet are introduced to the audience, leave the platform, get into separate helicopters, fly away, and eventually return. During their half-hour flight, visual and audio feeds of their playing, each instrument blending with the sound of an individual helicopter, are relayed to a control desk in the concert hall, and from there to video monitors and speaker systems in quad formation. The players have detailed and precisely timed individual parts, largely consisting of fricative tremolos rising and falling in pitch. The two components – string instruments and helicopters – are intended to represent similar whirring processes at opposite extremes of magnification. The helicopter pilots follow timed instructions on when to take off, when to change speed

[34] Jon Gertner, *The Idea Factory: Bell Labs and the Great Age of American Innovation* (New York, 2012), pp. 325–6.

and direction, and in what order to land. Before departing, players and pilots are interviewed about their expectations, and, on their return, assemble on the platform to be interviewed a second time about the experience, and take questions from the audience. These encounters are opportunities to reassure the public that the event has really taken place and not been faked in a movie studio. The entire episode is staged as music theatre in the style of a reality television production unfolding in an unedited, seamless continuum, open to the unexpected in various ways calculated to emphasize the unscripted nature of the event at a human level.

In conversation with Jonathan Cott in 1971, Stockhausen recalled experiences of flying over America on his first tour of American universities in late 1958. At that time,

> Most of the planes were propeller planes, and I was always leaning my ear – I *love* to fly, I must say – against the window, like listening with earphones directly to the inner vibrations. And though theoretically a physicist would have said that the engine sound doesn't change, it changed all the time because I was listening to all the partials within the spectrum. It was a fantastically beautiful experience. . . . And I really discovered the innerness of the engine sounds. . . . I had the feeling that I was visiting the earth and living in the plane. There were just very tiny changes of bluish colour and always this harmonic spectrum of the engine noise.[35]

Stockhausen is referring to the blended sound of transcontinental four-engine propeller planes from the 1950s, large passenger aircraft like the Lockheed Constellation or Douglas DC-6. Today, passengers boarding a commuter turboprop may experience a little of what Stockhausen describes, by leaning as he did against the window and listening to the frankly magical sound of propellers moving in and out of phase with one another, creating moiré-like interference effects.

Stockhausen's insistence on documentary reality speaks to a contemporary perception of world events experienced indirectly, in reported form, through radio, television, movies, personal phone, and the internet. Less than a decade after the premiere of *Helicopter String Quartet*, life in the financial district of New York was shattered in 2001 by the grotesque theatre of the destruction of the Twin Towers by hijacked passenger planes, an event witnessed in real time on cable television news channels across the United States. Later that very day the composer invited intense criticism, and cancellation of a festival of his music in Hamburg, for describing his impression of the Twin Towers attack to a roomful of excited press reporters as a work of art on a cosmic scale. In his

[35] Jonathan Cott, *Stockhausen: Conversations with the Composer* (London, 1974), p. 37.

youth during the war he had no doubt marvelled at news reports of Japanese kamikaze attacks on US battleships. To understand a response characterizing a choreographed act of massive destruction as art, one need only take note of the considerable number of classic works of art, preserved in monuments and galleries around the world, that celebrate war on the battlefield, at sea, and more recently in the air. While one may not assume that a composition in which members of a string quartet are loaded on to separate helicopters and fly away invariably has bad outcomes in mind, such a possibility inevitably adds dramatic tension to an event unfolding live and on camera, of musicians having to perform while squeezed uncomfortably into unsteady platforms hovering in mid-air. (Forcing musicians into the cramped space of a small helicopter may be explained as the composer's unconscious reaction to the communications industry practice of squeezing music into a frequency space so restricted it can barely survive transportation through the airwaves to the listener.) A sense of danger as well as loss of comfort also serves to concentrate the mind, along with the lingering possibility that something might go horribly wrong, so that at the end of the performance the audience is disposed to express a collective sigh of relief that the test – literally a rite of passage and potentially life-changing experience – has been safely completed.

String players may construe a half hour of virtually unrelieved 'scrubbing' back and forth – continuous tremolo is hardly the most attractive or eloquent of sounds – as a deliberate insult to the training and experience of those who dedicate themselves to a lifetime of art. In that sense, the composer's motive for the entire exercise could at best be excused metaphorically as a strategy for scrubbing away layers of tradition to restore an original sense of aesthetic purpose, in its way no less valid than cleaning away the accumulated dirt of centuries to reveal an old masterwork of art in vivid life and original colour. A half-hour exercise in rapidly bowing back and forth in partnership with a machine is bound in any case to open ears and minds to density and texture of bowing as authentic compositional variables, and awaken sensitivities to normally inaudible subtleties and shades of string tone revealed by near field microphones.

The mere presence of helicopters is a challenge to many, apart from the astringent nature of the music, which appears brutally constrained in comparison to the normal range of expression available to a classical string quartet. The challenge is to persuade an audience to feel justified in taking this work seriously, not only as an authentic musical experience, but as a genuine work of musical art firmly situated in the classical repertoire. To the question 'Is it music?' the answer is firmly yes. To the follow-up question, 'Is a helicopter to be treated as a musical instrument?' the answer again is sure, why not, it is a specifically musical sound as long as one knows how to use it. Finally, to the question, 'Is the *Helicopter String Quartet* readily identifiable as a genuine Stockhausen composition?' the answer is emphatically yes, absolutely: who else would attempt such a thing? All the same, there are those – perhaps even a majority – who consider the combination of engines and live instruments to be merely fanciful, ingenious, arbitrary, even perverse. Critics may yet object that music should not concern itself with the mundane world of science and technology. It has even been argued, not least by Stockhausen himself, that to talk about his music in this way is unhelpful, or misleading, because it exposes to plain sight an experience that should be utterly captivating, even mystical in nature. The issue of whether or what it is right and proper to talk about is addressed in a dialogue with the composer included in the Introduction to *Other Planets*. From such exchanges of opinion a reader may become aware of characteristic differences between English and German approaches to works of high cultural significance, which may help to explain why, in his lifetime, Stockhausen's music has appeared to attract more widespread attention in the English language press than in Germany itself. In Germany the challenge is to construct puzzles, while the English take delight in solving them. My own view is that great art endures on its merits, and the aim of a critic is certainly not to dispel or demystify the experience, but rather to identify the sacred inherent in the familiar.

In *Helicopter String Quartet* mechanical devices – helicopters – are employed as virtual timekeepers. A helicopter in flight is a kind of metronome, a mechanical conductor which the player has to follow. Tremolos of variable density rising up and down the scale also play a determining role in (say) the first movement of Mozart's Symphony No. 40 in G minor, a late work in which we hear an alert, but graceful, dance movement for string orchestra suddenly transformed into a virtual rainstorm, or overwhelmed by panic, the ensemble spontaneously erupting into dense noise. Such a descent into frictional noise is a mark of *Sturm und Drang* – 'Storm and Stress' – the late classical idiom intended to remind audiences of the superior power of Nature – and, by analogy, the present threat, to a late-eighteenth-century audience, of organized *human* nature rising in opposition to inherited structures of authority.

Mozart's contemporaries developed variable density as an expressive dimension in part to distinguish live from mechanically reproduced music. In the Introduction to the first movement of his Fourth Symphony, Beethoven alternates filled and empty measures, like a cell dividing, introducing life into the void to fashion an image of creation unfolding to the virtual tick of a metronome. For European audiences in the late eighteenth and early nineteenth centuries, the concept of variable density of activity gained acceptance as a by-product of the industrial age, a challenge to the classical image of divine authority controlling the flow of events, or powering a musical box, player piano, or steam-powered fairground organ programmed by punched cards. In adapting music to be performed by machines of limited power composers and listeners alike awakened to a new perception of musical time as the constant of which texture and density represent expressive variables. From a mechanical viewpoint, the intermittently repeated chords at the introduction of Beethoven's 'Waldstein' piano sonata make an obvious statement about variable density, since passages of alternating dense and sparse note content are not easy to reproduce at a constant speed on a mechanical instrument of strictly limited power. In the *Helicopter String Quartet*, constancy of speed is a given – a necessary safety consideration – entailed by an expressive intention of prolonged, uniformly textured playing, that each string player blend in with the sound of a helicopter to create an attractively iridescent tone quality. As Debussy's style of tone painting invites comparison with French impressionist art, so the abrasive texture of Stockhausen's tremolo strings finds a visual analogue in the dazzling interference patterns of the op art of Bridget Riley.

Helicopter String Quartet is a particularly austere example of music operating on two different scale magnifications at once, an idiom where the surface structure and shape of melodies – or even of manufactured tone qualities assembled on tape, as in *Kontakte* – reproduce in microcosm the rhythms and larger proportions of the whole. Stockhausen's short work *Jubiläum* (1977) is an interesting precursor example of an orchestral polyphony of multiple voices representing different degrees of magnification of the same melodic motif. In this occasional work, different layers of the composition are heard to speed up or slow down continuously, decelerating in the manner of a Synthi 100 data sequence from rapid tremolos to melodies of unequal note values, or mischievously accelerating from a solemn chorale to a rowdy texture. Bearing the idea of simultaneous layers of shifting acceleration and deceleration in mind, a bold juxtaposition of stringed instruments and helicopters makes unexpected sense, since both classes of instrument, bowed strings and flying machines, are fricative devices producing impulsive sounds at constantly varying timescales, in this case in the service of a controlled musical action consisting of continuous glides, rising and falling literally 'up and down the scale'.

The relation between tone quality, frequency, and complexity of impulsive tone structures had earlier been a topic of interest to Thomas Young and Hermann Helmholtz, nineteenth-century scientists who observed the effects of directing a stream of air through a siren, a rotating perforated disc, as a way of modelling the mechanism by which air released under pressure from the lungs interacts with the valve structure in the larynx and the resonant cavities of the vocal tract to produce vowel sounds of variable pitch and timbre. Coincidentally, when the tape-recorded sound of a speaking voice is slowed down with the aid of a voltage-controlled tape recorder, it too eventually bottoms out as the low, thudding sound of a passing helicopter – a noteworthy transformation with which Stockhausen was undoubtedly familiar from personal experience in the studio, and a species of transformation for which tape technology is essential.

Altering the timescale of experience is not a new idea. In the short story 'The New Accelerator' by H. G. Wells, published in 1904, an experimental biologist and his companion take a potion that speeds up their senses to such a degree that the sights and sounds of the world around them appear suspended in time, or in extreme slow motion. From a relativistic perspective, the string players in *Helicopter String Quartet* are taking part in a similar slow-motion experiment, as representatives of a perception of events on a human scale placed in a situation of observing and actively coming to terms with the larger-than-life scale of coordinated helicopter flight. The uniformly abrasive string texture is explained as 'coloration' of the sound of the helicopter rotors in motion as the aircraft manoeuvre up and down, their tone subtly changing in frequency and inner harmony. The agitated, continuous tremolos the players are obliged to maintain for most of their time aloft, combined with imagery of warped surfaces reaching upward into space, also call to mind the strident textures and idealized geometric surfaces of early computer-aided compositions by Iannis Xenakis. Impulsive repetitions are equally a feature of Stockhausen's 'Kathinkas Gesang' (1983–4) from the opera *Samstag aus LICHT*, in the IRCAM version which offsets a solo flute against a whirling, detonating tornado of computer-generated sound in continuously gliding rotation.

Historians of popular culture may imagine that the art of multi-channel mixing began in the 1960s with Phil Spector and his 'wall of sound' productions of the Ronettes and the Righteous Brothers – a technique of multi-channel tape layering evolved to create the impression of a wide-screen panorama passing through the needle's eye of a new generation of transistor radios. In fact, some of the earliest attempts at the multi-channel genre were created at the original mixing desk created in 1932 for the British Broadcasting Corporation at the request of Val Gielgud, chief producer for BBC Radio Drama. The Dramatic Control Panel came into being at a time when all radio transmissions, including radio plays, were broadcast live, a time when public acceptance of the radio medium as a credible source of information relied on an implicit understanding that everything a listener heard was real and, like the news and the weather, an event actually happening at the time it was heard. The BBC Dramatic Control Panel allowed the producer, *sight unseen*, to blend voices, sound effects, music, and added reverberation, all from separate studios, cued only with the aid of light signals. In effect, Stockhausen's *Helicopter String Quartet* recreates in exaggerated form a perception of the reality of radio drama productions from a past era when instant radio was the dominant communications medium and radio drama the most powerful and far-reaching of new art forms.

During the 1930s, the German firm BASF introduced magnetic-coated paper tape for storing audio in editable form, a new medium capable of being used to manipulate the sequence, and thereby influence a listener's perception of the sequence, and thus the apparent logic, of newsworthy events. Access to the new invention was strictly withheld from the rest of the world. During the war, morale-boosting 'Frontberichte' newscasts from radio stations in Cologne and Düsseldorf assured listeners in Germany of imminent victory, in broadcasts seemingly relayed live from the front line. In reality these mini-dramas were assembled on tape in the studio, and narrated against a backdrop of prerecorded sound effects of explosions and flying aircraft, sounds of a kind eventually to provide an emotional backdrop to the opera *Tuesday from LIGHT.*

Beginning in 1953, Stockhausen's professional life as an employee of Cologne Radio brought him in contact with a sophisticated older generation of balance engineers representing an established culture of manufactured reality assembled on audiotape. Against that background of manipulation of technology for propaganda and deception, a significant element of the drama of *Helicopter String Quartet* can be understood to lie in the irony of such a performance as an actual event: something that is happening in real time, not an illusion created on tape. Just as it had been for BBC drama producer Val Gielgud in 1932, the real-time production involved splitting up an ensemble into groups – players, voices, studio audience, producer, and technical support staff – and sending them off to separate studio locations while maintaining contact and coordinating their actions at a distance by radio link.

After his war service, in the late 1940s Stockhausen had enrolled as a music education student at the Cologne Music High School, whose newly appointed director was Hans Mersmann, a Béla Bartók and new music enthusiast finally permitted to resume teaching in 1947 following his abrupt dismissal from a teaching post at the Technical High School in Berlin in 1933, on account of his support of Schoenberg and his school. In politically uncertain times, Stockhausen seized the opportunity under Mersmann's watch to write his graduation thesis on the Bartók *Sonata for Two Pianos and Percussion*, even then a controversial work by the exiled Hungarian composer who died in New York in 1945. Sweeping glissandi play a significant role in Bartók's middle period and late works, such as the *Music for Strings, Percussion, and Celesta* and *Concerto for Orchestra*. In the third movement of Bartók's Second Violin

Concerto, composed in 1937, the soloist's impulsive tremolos up and down the scale are projected against a backdrop of sweeping and diving moves by the orchestra – an imagery of hectic instability suggestive of newsreel movie footage of fighter aircraft in mortal combat. Similar imagery of rising and falling frictional tone, offset against an unstable backdrop of musical detonations, is heard again in the melancholy final minutes of Stockhausen's *Kontakte*, whose tape-recorded sounds are artificial, in contrast to *Helicopter String Quartet* in which the sounds of both string quartet and helicopters are unquestionably real.

Stockhausen's lifelong fascination with rotary motion may have been triggered in 1952 in Paris, where he encountered *musique concrète*, a culture of multilayered sound effects blended from a plurality of turntables recycling pre-recorded sounds on acetate discs. For ease of use, disc-recorded sound effects of short duration, like a door slam, were routinely stored on separate grooves, each one a closed loop, in French a *sillon fermé*. One could alter the relative sharpness and weight of such pre-recorded effects by speeding up or slowing down these turntables within the range of about an octave, between 60 and 120 revolutions a minute, to alter the quality of sound from hard and crisp at high speed, to more sluggish, deeper, and foggier sounding at slower than normal speed. For greater precision of timing, Club d'Essai composers employed the *phonogène*, an ingenious multi-head tape delay machine invented by Jacques Poullin, a machine allowing a tape-recorded segment or sound to be precisely dilated or compressed in pitch by ratios corresponding to intervals of the equal tempered scale. At Cologne Radio, a tape transposition device called a Springer-machine was about to be approved as a mechanical aid to adjust the timing and internal tuning of tape-recorded programme content by minute degrees. Both methods of transformation led Stockhausen towards the idea of a music of continuous scale transformation extending across the continuum of frequency from rhythm in the infrasound to the limits of shimmering brilliance of effect in the ultrasound. By way of example, consider speeding up the tape of a composition such as *Drumming* by Steve Reich so that instead of listening for twenty-eight minutes the entire work is over in just half a minute; then making that half minute of tape into a loop and speeding it up even more. At a certain point, like a helicopter taking off, what started out as a slowly changing rhythm of beats in real time is transformed into a wavering tone whose specific timbre represents the transformational pattern of Reich's entire composition of twenty-eight minutes compressed into every waveform.

In mechanical terms, a tone of constant pitch is audible evidence of the efficiency with which a vibrating body is discharging superfluous energy into the atmosphere. As a multi-blade helicopter rotor gathers speed beyond twenty impulses per second a listener's perception of a periodic beat is overlaid by a continuous tone of rising pitch, a transformation on a human scale equivalent to increasing the speed of a tape loop to a point where a sequence of pulses blends into a continuous waveform. In the sound of a helicopter, however, several different elements are in play. One is the motor driving the rotor blades, which operates at its own speed represented by a continuous tone in the audible range of frequencies. A second ingredient is the rotor blades themselves, which relative to the engine are rotating considerably more slowly, but are capable of generating powerful low-frequency interference effects with the ground below and with nearby aircraft. A third factor is near field reverberation of the structure of the aircraft, a combination of internal resonances to which the airborne string quartet player is expected to react. Added to which, the note of the engine and the tone of the rotor blades, despite being widely separated in frequency, are coupled together mechanically so that as the engine note rises in pitch, the beat of the rotor blades increases in relation. An analogous acoustic effect can be heard near the beginning of the tape part of Stockhausen's *Kontakte* for electronic sounds, piano, and percussion. One hears a flap – flap – flap increasing in speed as the tape-recorded sound passes in rotation from speaker to speaker.

Making an audiovisual documentary of four helicopters flying off in different directions is already a demanding creative task in production terms, logistically and imaginatively. Whether or not the musical dimension is taken into account, such a project may still be appreciated by the general public as a work of technical art, as expressed in the video documentary by Frank Scheffer with the Arditti Quartet. That still leaves unanswered how such a work can be comfortably accommodated in the traditional repertoire of classical music in general, and the history of Western music in particular, in the sense of representing a perception of beauty in music originating within an established European tradition.

In the Futurist Manifesto published in 1913, the year of the premiere of Stravinsky's *Le sacre du printemps*, Luigi Russolo announced a new 'art of noises', declaring

> We must break out of this narrow circle of pure musical sounds, and conquer the infinite variety of noise-sounds. . . . Let us wander through a great modern city with our ears more attentive than our eyes, and distinguish the purring of motors (which breathe and pulsate with an indisputable animalism), the throbbing of valves, the pounding of pistons, the screeching of gears. . . . We must fix and regulate the harmonies and rhythms of these extraordinarily varied sounds . . . give definite gradation of pitch to the stronger and more

> predominant of these vibrations. . . . Thus certain noises produced by rotary motion may offer a complete ascending and descending chromatic scale by merely increasing or decreasing the speed of the motion.[36]

The Futurists were fascinated by piston engines and machines, in much the same way as viewers in the digital age are fascinated by transformers, improbable machines capable of reassembling themselves from sports cars of modest proportions into rampaging robot superheroes. The Futurists brought their innocent ears to bear on the novel piston-engine sounds of trucks, trains, tractors, and airplanes, and were entranced at the beauty and complexity of inner life of sounds of machines in motion, accelerating from a standing start, rising to a steady peak, then descending and stopping. In 1923, five years before Stockhausen was born, the composer Arthur Honegger painstakingly translated the sound of a record-breaking steam engine into music, in the symphonic movement *Pacific 2–3–1* for orchestra, destined in 1948 to become the soundtrack of a documentary movie depicting the express engine of the same name. Of particular interest in a conversation about helicopters is the way Honegger employs the tactile associations of bow on string to convey the high-friction noise of metal grinding against metal.

Pacific 2–3–1 is an example of a highly capable composer composing an art deco occasional piece celebrating a powerful machine, a poster image emblematic of high-speed travel, and a music the primary aesthetic interest of which is accurate representation of a massive steam engine building up speed, running at speed, then slowing down and coming to a stop. As a representation of musical form, the process sounds all too simple. But this, after all, is what engines do: they start, increase speed, slow down, and stop. In musical terms, the action of a railway journey consists of a beginning, middle, and end. What else is there? For a songwriter, a melody has to begin somewhere by finding a note, after which all it can do is go up or down, stay in the same place, or statistically speaking embark on a fractal combination of all three, and then stop, usually at roughly the point where it started. All the rest, as Stockhausen would say, is little details.

The invention of rhythm multiplexing as a specifically American phenomenon is associated with Joseph Schillinger, a Russian émigré and teacher regarded with awe by John Cage and Earle Brown. His two-volume treatise *The Schillinger System of Musical Composition* (1945–6) includes helpful instructions on inventing and combining multiple rhythms, said to have influenced Schillinger's pupil George Gershwin (the composer of 'Fascinating

[36] Luigi Russolo, 'The Art of Noises: Futurist Manifesto'. In Nicolas Slonimsky ed., *Music Since 1900* (New York, 1949), pp. 642–8.

Rhythm') along with a younger generation of songwriters including Burt Bacharach, composer of the rhythmically teasing 'Planes and Boats and Planes' and 'Do You Know the Way to San Jose'. Nor is Stockhausen the first composer to treat the members of a string quartet as independent voices. In his String Quartet No. 1 (1951) Elliott Carter followed mentor Charles Ives in synchronizing the notated parts exactly on the printed page while requiring the players to give the impression of performing totally independently – a neat idea in itself and philosophically the opposite of a John Cage creation in which there is nothing specific to coordinate the players' actions except a shared space and the time of day. (Interestingly, Cage's own *String Quartet in Four Parts* (1950) is exactly notated.)

In Carter's string quartet, which also acknowledges the hand-punched polymetrical compositions for player piano of Conlon Nancarrow, the four parts coordinating at different tempi also create an impression of commuters in separate vehicles driving along the same expanse of motorway at different speeds. It is the composer's way perhaps of saying that there is more to life than one timescale of experience, a version of the authentically American view that citizens and other animals share the gift to be free to move and respond to the world in independent and approximate rather than exactly coordinated gestures. For his String Quartet No. 2 (1959) Carter seated the four players farther apart on the concert platform, as if to exaggerate their individuality in spatial as well as contrapuntal terms, an act of separation effectively slowing coordination and also inhibiting eye contact between the players. Following such precedents, placing the four musicians in separate helicopters could be seen as simply extending the principle a stage further, a gesture in the spirit of Henry Brant dispersing his players on different canal boats in his Amsterdam composition *Fire on the Amstel* (1984). Whether on the concert platform or in the air, technically the act of physical separation of players is open to interpretation as a radio production trait corresponding to the superimposition of multiple inputs from separate microphones – a compound monophonic aesthetic equally characteristic of Boulez's *Le marteau* (1953–5) and Stockhausen's *Zeitmasse* (1955–6).

Historically, *Helicopter String Quartet* is music about going up in the air. Air is the region of angels and fire-breathing dragons; it is also the realm of sound and hearing. In a medieval sense, to be lifted in spirit is to become one with the angels. The world of art music contains a multitude of examples specifically about rising up in the air, and sound travelling through the air as a spatial dimension. A tiny example is the 'Et Misericordia' from Monteverdi's *Vespers* of 1610, a choral setting of a text from the scriptures about the spirit being raised to hope. The choir begins in a subdued, low register, brightening in tone as the music rises in pitch until the treble voices appear to encounter a 'glass ceiling' or limit above which they are unable to ascend. After a moment's pause, the verse begins again, voices rising from the depths a second time, to the previous high note. Here the treble melody briefly stalls: then, in a moment of magic, passes through the glass ceiling and flies away, an effect of high emotion achieved in the deftest of terms, and a gesture aided by the fact that the choir voices are arranged in tiers, the basses at ground level and tenors, altos and trebles at successively higher levels, signifying that as the melody ascends in pitch, it is also rising upward in real space.

Flying above the earth became a socially desirable experience in Mozart's lifetime, following the Montgolfier brothers' successful launch in 1783 of a hot air balloon made of reinforced wallpaper fabric. The eyes of late-eighteenth-century society turned towards the clouds. Landscape artists John Constable and J.M.W. Turner lifted their gaze from ground-based features of the natural landscape to focus on scarcely tangible airborne effects such as air pollution over Venice, fire at sea, or storm-clouds gathering over the English Channel. In the late nineteenth century, cellist and composer Friedrich Grützmacher took advantage of the extended range of his instrument to transform the first of a medley of Boccherini's late-eighteenth-century cello concerto movements catalogued as No. 9 in B flat to create a humorous impression of being raised up in a balloon at reckless speed, disappearing behind a cloud, then descending to earth with a bump.

For Beethoven, the superhuman power of the atmosphere is closer to the charge famously demonstrated in 1752 by Benjamin Franklin flying a kite into a thundercloud to prove that lightning and electricity were essentially the same. In the third movement of Beethoven's No. 6 'Pastoral' Symphony the composer depicts the mood of a gathering storm with great finesse. Even though his subject is the power of Nature, not helicopters, Beethoven's instrumentation and textures are uncannily similar to Stockhausen's tremolo strings, rising up the scale, hovering, the bolt of lightning, then descending to earth. At the climax of Beethoven's storm, the point where the piccolo is heard, a cross-fade to the climax (at 26′ 52″) of the Arditti Quartet recording of *Helicopter String Quartet* blends the two works, composed nearly two centuries apart, in seamless agreement.

In similar acknowledgement, pioneer *avion* designer Clément Ader's bold assertion of having achieved heavier-than-air powered flight for the glory of France in 1890 may have provoked Nicolai Rimsky-Korsakov, at the time a serving officer in the Imperial Russian Navy, to compose a charming miniature for orchestra known in English as 'Flight of the Bumble-Bee'. Like Ader's flying machine, the bumble-bee is a body whose wings appear too small in scale to support its relative bulk in controlled continuous flight. Musically speaking, Rimsky's melody more closely resembles the sound of an angry blowfly trying desperately to escape, than an amiable bumble-bee grizzling benignly over a flower. More to the point, the continuous buzzing tone of a bumble-bee in flight, as of any insect, is bound to remain relatively constant, despite sudden fluctuations in loudness and changes of direction, in that sense resembling a tiny, speeded-up version of a Stockhausen helicopter. Rimsky-Korsakov's orchestral vignette is a miniature of genius, a flying Fabergé creation of gold and precious stones. The composer evokes the insect's erratic movement back and forth, passing from the edgier sound of violins at the front of the platform to softer-toned flutes at the rear in realistic imitation of the front to back motion of a real insect in flight.

Less than a minute and a half long, the Prelude to Stravinsky's late masterwork *Requiem Canticles* (1966) is yet another Russian miniature in which a *ripieno* string orchestra chugs along in piston-like even beat harmonies while four solo voices (violin, viola, cello, and bass) join one by one in elevated conversation above the traffic. Composed seventeen years before *Helicopter String Quartet*, Stravinsky's own farewell gesture is curiously similar in implication, a meditation on taking to the air, thudding strings imitating the rotors of helicopters in flight overhead, and the solo quartet the voices of pilots giving and receiving directions. Cultural historians may recall Jimi Hendrix's blazing appearance at Woodstock in 1969, improvising an extended, abrasive guitar riff on the sound of a helicopter raid on Vietnamese resistance fighters to the strains of a distorted US anthem.

Associations of helicopters with thoughts of self-destruction and revenge are largely absent from *Helicopter String Quartet*, though one has to acknowledge an ongoing sense of clear and present danger, including the risk of damaging precious instruments – yet another reason why Stockhausen's individual parts for string quartet are drawn in terms simple enough for the players not to require their most expensive instruments. An impressive takeaway of the Birmingham UK performances of *Helicopter String Quartet* in 2012, marking the week-long British premiere of the opera *Mittwoch aus LICHT*, was audience appreciation of the professionalism and commitment to service of the string players and their pilots, in performances of a demanding precision intended to take all participants out of their normal comfort zones.

On first hearing the Arditti premiere recording on compact disc in 1998 I sensed straight away that this was a ceremony of leave-taking, and the composer was saying goodbye. I feared the opera cycle might never be finished, and this work might be his last. As the quartet and helicopters return to earth, their descending scales merge over the final few minutes in a shadowy but intensely emotional *tonal* progression evoking the solemn pace and inexorable decline of the ground bass to 'Dido's Lament' from *Dido and Aeneas* by Purcell, a setting of the lyric 'When I am laid, am laid in earth'. I have no idea at all if Stockhausen was thinking of Purcell when he began composing a work for string quartet and four helicopters; but I can imagine the connection coming spontaneously to the composer's mind at the mixing desk, reinforcing an underlying impression that a work about flying up in the air is preoccupied at some level with thoughts of mortality.

Compared with the clinical precision and somewhat antiseptic computer-generated tonalities of Boulez's *Répons*, the intensely tactile tones and textures of *Helicopter String Quartet* are open to be read as a stark criticism by Stockhausen of the digital medium and its advantages. Equally stark is the contrast between an aesthetic based on numbers corresponding to instantaneous states, and an analogue medium grounded in interval relations and continuity of change – in other words, a moral defence *both* of Schoenberg's method based on contiguous note relations *and* Nadia Boulanger's practice of 'the long line'. By definition, the flight portion of the performance is an unavoidably seamless continuum. There is no role for a conductor. Coordination in flight between players is effected by pre-recorded click tracks. In principle the entire episode is totally controlled, yet at the same time inherently unpredictable at every level. The before and after episodes, in which players and pilots are interviewed and questions taken from the public, are technically 'happenings' in the Cageian sense of public events in which anything may happen, but in this instance occasions in which the sense of ritual exerts a powerful control on the attention and behaviour of the audience.

A helicopter, by the way, is also known as a 'chopper' because of the chopping sound made by the rotor blades. A 'chopper' is also the name of a piece of analogue studio equipment otherwise known as a noise gate or impulse generator. It works a little bit like an electronic siren. A classic siren consists of a rotating disc with holes through which compressed air is forced, making a sound like a wailing female voice, but a great deal louder. Sirens were initially adopted by Edgar Varèse in 1924 for the composition *Hyperprism*. The story goes that Varèse was rehearsing *Hyperprism* with a group of musicians in his New York penthouse apartment with its windows open when their attention was caught by a fire engine passing in the street below, sounding a newfangled siren in place of the traditional ringing bell. Varèse stopped the rehearsal, grabbed his coat, and hastened to the fire station to request the loan of two instruments for his new composition from a bemused fire chief.

The violin family, including viola and cello, are friction instruments, their sound principally produced by rubbing a rosined bow at right angles across one or more stretched strings of variable length. The slip-stick action of bow on string excites a typically sawtooth waveform owing to adhesion of the bow hair alternately dragging and releasing the string, action repeated many times a second. Viewed under the microscope, the effect of slip-stick action is to add an impulsive texture to the string tone at high speed. The combined dynamic of string tone and frictional noise of the bow gives the violin family a more malleable and public character in comparison to the quiet reserve of the baroque viol consort, whose bows are shorter, bow action more discreet, and tone lighter and purer.

In his Futurist Manifesto, Russolo writes of the possibility of harnessing the sounds of machines to create a music of continuously rising and falling harmonies. In combining a string quartet with four helicopters, and asking the string players to play along and blend in with the sound of the engines and rotor blades, Stockhausen appears to be taking the Futurists at their word and creating a work in which the string instruments and helicopters are not simply duetting alongside one another, but intensifying the rich background tones of the machines to bring out their underlying musical quality.

That being the case, in the *Helicopter String Quartet* the string players are assuming the roles of tunable filters or artificial enhancers of coloured noise produced by the helicopters. How that works has previously been demonstrated in Stockhausen's seventy-minute composition *Stimmung* (1968) for six unaccompanied voices. In German, the word *Stimmung* means 'agreement', and also 'tuning' in the sense of fine-tuning a radio to a desired channel, or attaining an ideal state of mind for receiving messages from the beyond. On hearing *Stimmung* for the first time – the work Boulez described rather patronisingly to a reporter as 'the endless chord, how terribly German' – a listener may have the impression of hearing a gramophone recording stuck permanently in a closed groove. *Stimmung* is a study in close, and also *true* (that is, Pythagorean) harmony based on a single six-part chord of the ninth – harmonics 2, 3, 4, 5, 7, 9 – in the key of B flat. While the chord remains outwardly frozen, the constituent partial tones represented by individual voices continuously fade in and out of focus, at times shaped into words in slow motion, as if the singers were radio channels tuned to the same or related frequencies. Not only is the harmonic structure of the ensemble constantly in flux, changing shape, but from time to time individual voices within the group drift away, lose their place, or otherwise rise to the surface, inflecting words and syllables in the close-microphone style of a barbershop quartet, to a point where the singing ceases to be about words and becomes a play of abstract shapes. A performance in Amsterdam in 1969 was disrupted by disappointed protesters who took umbrage at having to listen patiently for seventy minutes to a work they had expected to be less intense, more easygoing in tone, Stockhausen's version of 'make love not war'.

After *Mixtur* (1966), a Stockhausen composition employing ring modulators with mixed success to transform live instrumental sound, and *Mantra* for two pianos (1970) in which filtered and heavily compressed piano tone is effectively modulated by sweep frequency oscillators, it is not difficult to recognize *Helicopter String Quartet* as another work in the same conceptual space, since the basic mechanisms for modulation are in place, and the string players are instructed to blend in with the sound of their respective aircraft. Perhaps mindful of previous technical difficulties, the composer has assigned ultimate responsibility for the composite sound to a sound controller on the ground, the UK Birmingham premiere employing a substantial barricade of audio and video apparatus separating the performers in flight from the audience sheltered at ground level.

In comparison with traditional performance practice where close-knit members of a string quartet face one another on the concert platform and interact by sound and gesture to a high degree of unanimity, *Helicopter String Quartet* places ultimate responsibility for richness of blended effect on the balance engineer at the control desk rather than relying on the performers or natural acoustic of the auditorium. As in the battle scenes of Stockhausen's opera *Dienstag aus LICHT*, and throughout the turbulence of *Cosmic Pulses* (2007), the desired dramatic effect of reproducing extreme low-frequency sounds at intensities capable of setting the walls and floor of an auditorium palpably in motion to dramatic effect, can be vitiated in practice by practical compromises – not least, public safety regulations – regarding the employment of subaudio frequencies powerful enough to set an entire auditorium in stomach-churning vibration. It may be exciting in principle to imagine being trapped underneath the sound of four helicopters hovering a few feet overhead, but in practice an overhead sound field of equivalent intensity is apt to inflict serious damage on the physical body.

Whereas the role of very low frequencies in normal hearing is still not widely understood, infrasound nevertheless remains a real and significant aspect of the professional knowledge of a pipe organ builder and tuner in relation to how a near subaudio fundamental tone interacts with higher frequencies to draw them into harmonious alignment. While lower notes normally require greater energy and proportionally larger instruments, an apparatus of larger size does not always entail a more powerful tone in human terms. Consider a renaissance consort of matching recorders, designed to produce precisely similar waveforms, varying in size from an eight-foot contrabass to a sopranino of a foot in length, among which counterintuitively it is the smallest instrument of the ensemble that sounds the loudest and most piercing, while the largest remains barely audible. Among modern orchestral instruments the contrabass clarinet is so low in pitch that in isolation its tone is virtually inaudible, but as anchor to the family of clarinets in a symphony orchestra it adds palpable depth and stability. In isolation the tone of a 32-foot organ pipe is virtually impossible to detect, but as pedal point to the opening fanfare of Richard Strauss's orchestral tone poem *Also sprach Zarathustra* it adds significantly to the weight and depth of the full orchestra.

In separating members of the string quartet from one another, taking them off the ground and up in the air, and sending them in different directions, Stockhausen has removed them from their natural arena on the platform, a resonating surface to which the cello is normally anchored by its spike, a mechanism for communicating low-frequency signals to the ensemble as a tactile guide to total harmonization. Imposing such extreme degrees of separation on a string quartet in individual helicopters obliges the operator at the mixing desk not only to monitor the blended tone of each player with its designated helicopter in real time during flight, but to assume responsibility for the blend of all four players and machines for listeners on the ground.

Such a plan assumes a rationale allowing the four helicopter sounds to influence one another directly, and a mechanism to realise a pattern of mutual interference potentially analogous to the experience the composer encountered on his travels as a passenger in a four-propeller airplane while leaning against the window and listening to the sound of engines moving in and out of phase with one another. The critical difference in *Helicopter String Quartet* is how to reproduce the acoustic sensation of four engine vibrations interacting, given that the four helicopters are not physically connected. The effect Stockhausen described in conversation with Jonathan Cott in 1974 has to refer to the vibrations of four propellers conducted through the same metal structure. Only by passing through the same rigid frame are the vibrations of each engine able to interact directly to produce the iridescent shifts of timbre that resemble the interplay of voices of *Stimmung*. The same richness and detail of musical interaction cannot be controlled, or even guaranteed to occur spontaneously among aircraft that are physically separated, unless perhaps all four helicopters are hovering uncomfortably close to one another, or near the ground in formation directly above the listener.

So for the time being, ultimate answers to integrating the sounds of the string quartet, individually with their designated helicopters, thereafter collectively at the mixing desk in the concert hall, remain literally up in the air, whether or not a recording or performance can be made to work satisfactorily from a technical perspective. Instinctively one imagines intermodulation of the four signals to be achievable in a concert hall setting by extracting the low frequencies from all four aircraft at 64-foot wavelengths corresponding to the major dimensions of the auditorium itself. Not only to preserve the personal audio signature of each individual aircraft, but in some way coupling them to the auditorium structure to allow all four sets of vibrations to interact. Maintaining control of four powerful subwoofers, radiating frequencies at intensities hazardous to audience well-being, may not be easy to achieve, even with industrial vibrators. Intense pressure waves below the range of normal hearing, in the bandwidth used by elephants and whales to communicate over vast distances at wavelengths of thirty feet or more, are apt in contained situations to interfere embarrassingly with the body's natural biorhythms and safety mechanisms – incontinence triggers exploited to mischievous effect in the late 1970s by the punk band Throbbing Gristle under lead singer Genesis P-Orridge.

On a string piano, as you go higher in pitch, the string gets shorter, and to compensate for loss of vibrating length the number of strings assigned to an individual note increases; as you go towards the bass, the strings increase in length, and become heavier, denser, and fewer. There is a necessary power asymmetry between bass and treble, left hand and right hand. Low or high, however, the same amount of energy is required to depress a piano key and make a sound. The lower the note, the fewer vibrations per second, fewer divisions of energy, and greater amount of energy expended in each cycle. For his final version of *Les Noces*, Stravinsky reduced the power resources of a symphony orchestra to just four pianos and a smattering of percussion. Four pianos were required not only to handle multiple parts, but also to generate a power and depth of sound equal to the scale of a concert hall and choir. Until recently, the lowest frequencies of a music recording would be filtered out because on a vinyl disc they tended to make a stylus skip uncontrollably, as well as draining undue amounts of domestic power, shaking the house, and disturbing the neighbours. Instead of four grand pianos, imagine a helicopter, multiplied by four, the sound of each rotor issuing from its own subwoofer delivering the equivalent power of a jackhammer to every corner of the concert chamber.

But for Stockhausen in 1993, the arrival of digital recording signified that those low frequencies could be left in place. We know that Stockhausen intended to take advantage of very low frequencies precisely because works such as the computer-generated tornado of 'Kathinkas Gesang' and the battle scenes of *Dienstag aus LICHT* specifically demand them. Using low frequencies to move sounds about in unpredictable ways was a tactic noted by Stockhausen's mentor Werner Meyer-Eppler in a 1955 paper published in *Die Reihe I*, but never deliberately implemented in practice. So-called 'aleatoric modulation' took advantage of the possibility of extending the audio signal into the subaudio region where the *same* low-frequency signal emitted from multiple speakers in different places might be expected to give rise to unpredictable interference patterns appearing to wander about the room. Stockhausen returns to this very idea one final time in *Cosmic Pulses*, his last major electronic composition. Here again the result, while compelling, does not altogether succeed, partly because, instead of following Meyer-Eppler and employing natural intermodulation, the composer has attempted to counter any uncertainty of effect by manually shaping each layer and part layer at the mixing desk.

In *Helicopter String Quartet* what I take to be the composer's intention – consistent with the composer's objections to aircraft from a nearby military base flying low over his home in rural Kürten, not to mention the noisy attentions of a neighbour's pet parrot invading his private space – would have been to use the helicopters as sources of very low frequencies to generate interference effects either in the air or conducted into the structure of an auditorium, the string quartet meanwhile interacting with the changing harmonies circulating in the air among the higher partials of helicopter tone. In turn, that level of specialization implies dedicated oversight of the pickup mechanisms installed within the aircraft and the structures on the ground where the same vibrations are retransmitted, safety and structural considerations requiring equipment robust enough to relay essential low-frequency information.

After many years of studying Stockhausen's music, while maintaining a corresponding relationship with the composer, an observer might be expected to develop a sixth sense of how his mind was working, or at least how to intuit his intentions in unexpected situations. To the objection that there is no evidence of the composer thinking in this way and that because there is no evidence, therefore there is nothing to criticize and any criticism is at best empty speculation, my only answer is that as long as we collaborated I would let him know in advance what I thought, and he would correct any errors of fact.

Now that the art of music has become entangled with rapidly evolving technologies of recording and computer processing of sound, new challenges have arisen to explain and reconcile classic conventions of music with the practical realities of audio processing. Similar technical issues also arise in relation to works by Boulez, Cage, Berio, and Ligeti, and examples of electronic music from the era of Ernst Krenek and Herbert Eimert. Recognition and remediation of discrepancies or disconnects between what a composing method or choice of instrumentation may suggest, and the message a piece of music delivers, however bizarre, should actually be regarded as the norm rather than the exception. The art of interpretation is not just about making a new work sound good, but requires a composer's intentions to be evaluated not in an aesthetic vacuum, but in terms of the possibilities his choices of material expose to consideration, and on that basis of possibilities to decide what has been successfully accomplished or omitted. This is the same whether the composer is a Stockhausen, or Mozart, or Bach, or Beethoven. The mistake is assuming that what is written on the page is all there is to be said. An interpreter is more than an assembly line worker. At times, bringing a piece to life demands the contribution of an experienced engineer: even at times, a paramedic.

3 *Cosmic Pulses*

> At the Brussels World Fair of 1958 there were already television screens 1.5 metres square on show representing the domestic television of the future. . . . I imagine the television of the future being in a special room with a spherical screen extending at least 270 degrees around and above the viewer, who will sit in a special chair in the centre. Image and sound will be transmitted in three dimensions.[37]

Traditional concert music and associated studio recording techniques are predicated on fixed tonal and spatial relationships. In ballet or opera, characters in costume move to accompanying music expressing the dynamics of motion, while musicians and audience members sit relatively still. A concert hall is an enclosure of fixed and acoustically stable and predictable dimensions; in a studio, microphones for recording and speakers for playback occupy fixed locations and vantage points.

In real life, however, movement is key. Things change. People and sounds do not stay in one place. Objects move from here to there as we wait; or as the listener moves, the acoustic environment rotates as a whole; often both at once. Among the most complicated of acoustic experiences routinely encountered in the city is to be standing at a busy high street intersection while waiting for the lights to change. Street traffic in continuous polyphony passes to left and right, moving at different speeds and distances; vehicles and people starting and stopping, singly and in groups, heading in different directions, the whole like a river in flood, the 'Beautiful Blue Danube' of musical metaphor. As any one ingredient of a flow of traffic changes position, its audio spectrum relative to the listener alters in subtle, but meaningful, ways related to the Doppler effect: changes which for the sake of simplicity can be described as red- and blue-shifting. To the waiting observer, the sound of an approaching vehicle is compressed and lifted in frequency, whereas the wave train of a motor accelerating away is stretched and sounds lower in pitch. The whirring of a piston engine issues periodic ripples into the surrounding air which at a certain rate of recurrence are transformed in human hearing from a pulsating rhythm to

[37] Karlheinz Stockhausen, *Stockhausen on Music* (London, 1989), pp. 146–7.

a musical tone. The art deco era celebrated streamlined speed. Imitation Doppler effects were introduced as a special effect of big band jazz, in group breaks caught on newsreel footage of choruses of trumpets, trombones, or saxophones taking turns to rise to their feet and swoop their instruments from right to left while playing choo-choo harmonies. As their sources move, real-life tones such as the sound of an airplane passing overhead are subject to complex internal phase changes, but the formula governing the process of change, a combination of speed, wavelength, and distance, remains the same for any sound, however complex its internal structure.

Composed in 2007, *Cosmic Pulses* is Stockhausen's ultimate statement in the electronic medium.[38] For a number of reasons I believe the composer knew it would be his last attempt, the summation of a life of inquiry into the nature of sounds in rotary motion. The work was completed in a rush. In many ways, notably in terms of the sound material, which is very basic, the music remains a sketch: a massive rotating sound mass, composed in twenty-four separately spinning frequency layers. Ascending from bass to treble, the layers accumulate gradually to twenty-four, then vacate upward one by one in an upward spiral that in the end vanishes abruptly. An audience may imagine experiencing the sensation of falling headlong into a black hole, or, if one is an optimist, being carried aloft on the whirlwind like Dorothy in *The Wizard of Oz*.

A hurricane or rotating air mass is an effect of a natural imbalance between temperature layers in the atmosphere, tipped into motion by the earth's rotation, which moves progressively faster towards the equator. The spinning current that results spirals upwards and generates a powerful electrical charge. By contrast, a black hole is a local concentration of gravitation creating an imbalance in spacetime. The rotational process that results spirals downward or inward, leading to the extinction of reality as we know it – or again, if one is an optimist, creating a wormhole emerging either into another universe entirely, or into our own universe at a remote point in time and space. Such grand cosmic associations are in keeping with the composer's superhuman imagination, while intimating an underlying agenda or consciousness of imminent rapture. Stockhausen had previously sought to replicate the experience of being caught up in a hurricane in a version of 'Kathinkas Gesang' created in 1983–4 at IRCAM, in that instance taking advantage of the computing power of the 4 C processor to conjure into being dense rotating composites of separate, but coordinated, harmonic layers, each with its own Doppler effect.[39]

[38] Robin Maconie, *Other Planets* (Lanham, MD, 2016), pp. 499–502.

[39] Karlheinz Stockhausen, Nr. 91 *Cosmic Pulses*. 13th Hour of *KLANG* (2006–07), www.stockhausen.org.

The dynamics of fluid flow are of interest to makers of musical instruments and of fundamental concern to aerodynamics engineers and designers, applying to the design of pipes and ducts conducting fluids, passive bodies such as aircraft moving through a current of air at speed, flows of people traffic in an airport or shopping mall, and in a different sense to the design of rotating bodies and cavities such as turbines and propellers which generate thrust in order to create movement. Music has an interest in the dynamics of fluid flow because among the oldest surviving musical instruments known to archaeology are bone flutes with clearly defined fingerholes, relics that clearly indicate an interest in the modelling and manipulation of an airflow within a confined space or duct. Intuitively, a stone age flutist was acquiring the art of regulating an airflow within a resonant cavity at a critical pressure point where the excess ventilated as tone fluctuates in dynamic, but stable, relation to the pressure introduced from an external mouth or bellows. The interest of such feedback processes in a primitive sense is of being able to model, and, by implication, takes control over a force of nature. It is pure science. In a musical sense, it is effort rewarded by the pleasure of converting a chaotic flow of air into a periodic, stable current of pressure pulses audible as a tone of constant pitch. Among the attractions of transforming a chaotic flow of energy into an audibly structured flow is that the tone that mysteriously results is beautiful in itself; but more to the point, the efficiency of the process is such that the resulting tone is able to carry over a greater distance than the voice under its own power. Employing a flute as an instrument of alarm is a practical and more energy-efficient mode of communication in the open air than singing or shouting, and more reliable in practice because the pipe being rigid vibrates in a predictable fashion compared to the voice, which relies on a combination of stiff and soft tissue.

It follows as a matter of principle that any *musical* composition inquiring into the nature of fluid flow and rotational processes is attached to an ancient tradition of studies in time and motion connecting the art of music with the origins of science and technology in general. To a listener experiencing the stunning 'flying saucer' arrival and departure moments of Stockhausen's 1977 electronic cantata *Sirius* – localized interference effects created by rotating a complex signal at high speed around a circular formation of eight speaker channels – it appears altogether logical that the sacred ceremonies for which stone circles such as Stonehenge were erected in the distant past must have been created with another ancient musical instrument in mind: a bull-roarer, a whirring, growling aerofoil of hard wood shaped like a propeller blade. When this object is rotated horizontally at high speed overhead at the end of a long cord, the resulting helicopter-like disturbance of air is bound to generate a magical pattern of acoustical standing waves by reflection from the inward facing surfaces of a surrounding circle of vertical stones.

On first hearing, *Cosmic Pulses* resembles an artist's representation of turbulence in nature of the kind recognized in the depiction of a storm or waterfall by a Turner or Petrus van der Velden. Self-evidently, *Cosmic Pulses* is a manufactured turbulence, and not a naturally occurring event. Turbulence in nature is a self-regulating process that is triggered when an excess of energy is introduced to a resisting cavity or conduit, like air under pressure to a pipe or flute. Among the examples of fluid flow described in James Gleick's *Chaos* is the special case of a fluid trapped between rotating inner and fixed outer cylinders, a situation spontaneously giving rise to a layered structure known as a Couette-Taylor flow.[40] A serially determined composition of up to twenty-four layers in simultaneous multiple rotation introduces an element of aesthetic play, or exploratory inquiry, to an otherwise natural process. In comparison to the passive 'flying saucer' moments of *Sirius*, the eight-channel turbulence of *Cosmic Pulses* asks to be considered, not simply as musical content for which the speakers provide a delivery system, but rather as the by-product of a complex of actively oscillating energies of varying amplitude in continuous interaction with a resonating container of fixed dimensions, such as an organ pipe. In this case, the container is the auditorium itself.

In Stockhausen's earlier tape works *Kontakte* and *Sirius*, blocks of complex, contrasting sound subject to multichannel rotation give rise to transient effects of mutual reinforcement and cancellation arising at wavelengths corresponding to the physical distances between opposing speakers, illusory effects varying with disconcerting precision according to frequency content, speed of rotation from speaker to speaker, orientation of the listener, and dimensions of the room. In *Cosmic Pulses*, by contrast, layers of similar tone material are set in independent rotation at different speeds, amounting to an organized polyphony of interval relations, wavelengths, speaker combinations, and periodicities. Here as in any compositional process the outcome of which cannot be totally predicted, the composer's strict adherence to serial protocols ensures that while the resulting complexity is guaranteed to provide a rich experience for all listeners, any unexpected outcome of special interest to science can be pinpointed to a precisely quantifiable combination of variables.

Given that *Cosmic Pulses*' twenty-four-layer complex of whirls and eddies is an intellectual construct based on aesthetic speculation and not an impression or imitation of a natural process, the impact of witnessing such a marvel of dynamic but stable multiple rotations may be compared to the visual wonder

[40] James Gleick, *Chaos: Making a New Science* (London, 1988), pp. 128–9.

of observing the interlocking multiple gears of an early pendulum clock in coordinated action. After contemplating the works of a mechanical timepiece of intermeshing cogwheels powered by weights, the fourteenth-century philosopher Jean Buridan was moved to conclude that the universe was maintained in stable and harmonious orbital motion not by God but by gravity. From a twenty-first-century perspective, *Cosmic Pulses* can be reviewed as an exercise in modelling the music of the spheres, a controversial assertion of human science as an alternative to divine will expressed in a mechanism for regulating and controlling the flow of cosmic time.

Whether sounds are natural or artificial in origin, the key to continuity in rotation, or any distributive process, is a singular and consistent power source. In the language of music, the unifying basis of harmony is identified with the power of the keynote or tonic, and for timbre, reinforcement of partial tones vibrating in step with the fundamental. Problems arise for the disposal of energy in vibrating structures forced to rotate at critical energies. A wineglass shattering in the presence of a pure tone, or a suspension bridge that collapses in response to the resonance set in motion by marching feet, or shaken by a passing gale, does so from an accumulation of vibrational feedback and associated stress that at a critical point is obliged to discharge explosively rather than gradually and safely. The makers of church bells understood this principle. The partial vibrations of a classic bell are inharmonic by design, forming an acoustic partnership in difference allowing each component to continue oscillating indefinitely and unopposed – a decoherence effect poetically conveyed in the isorhythmic piano part of Messiaen's 'Liturgie de Cristal', the first movement of *Quartet for the end of time*, in which a repeating cycle of durations is out of synch with its associated cycle of harmonies. Varying the thickness of metal not only protects a bell from cracking under the repeated action of the clapper, but alleviates the effects of harmonic stress by allowing the ensuing pattern of vibration to dissipate unevenly and over a longer period of time, in the process creating interesting inner fluctuations that cause the tone at a distance to sound voice-like.

Control issues relating to the coordination and management of multiple rotating layers at different speeds in acoustic space, along with technical issues of maintaining continuity of sounds moving at speed between speakers, are important structural subtexts of *Cosmic Pulses,* a work plainly devised to enable complexity to override aesthetic issues of instrumentation and finish. The unvarnished, industrial tone quality throughout the work is an additional clue to the composer's priorities at the time, a sense of urgency sharply conveyed in Richard Toop's fly on the wall observations of Stockhausen's concurrent rehearsals with a team of young synthesizer operators in the preparation of

'Sonntags Abschied', the finale of *Sonntag aus LICHT.* The composer set his assistants the outwardly straightforward task of developing and agreeing on a vocabulary of speechlike inflections based on the lyrics of 'Hoch-Zeiten', the central ceremony of Sunday's opera. Thirty years previously, following the success of *Stimmung*, a work in which six vocalists singing into microphones play the role of live synthesizers, for the 1971 composition *Sternklang* Stockhausen had enlisted a team of assistants including Roger Smalley and Tim Souster to perform the directly comparable task of inflecting the names of star constellations using portable EMS analogue synthesizers – a challenge achieved, as the record shows, with relative ease. Then, after completing *Sirius* in 1977, a sequencer-led composition created on the ageing Synthi 100 at Cologne Radio, Stockhausen opted to delegate future responsibility for timbre creation to assistants Simon Stockhausen and Antonio Pérez Abellán, by 2006 becoming heavily dependent on external help in adapting to a new generation of Kurzweil equipment with whose programming protocols and limitations he was no longer familiar, or indeed interested.[41]

Refinements of timbre play little or no role in *Cosmic Pulses*, whose core rationale of a structure of multiple periodicities is assumed by default to generate a cascade of spontaneous interactions arising from a calculatedly overwhelming number and variety of rotational combinations. The total effect may be compared to an action painting by Jackson Pollock, a gestural art trading a traditional appreciation of the artist's skill in imitating nature on a human scale for the thrill and sense of awe at the dynamics of nature on the scale of a nuclear event depicted in slow motion with the implacable consistency of a detonating body depicted in wave upon wave of interlacing patterns of droplets of contrasting colour.

Since the 1930s, the unpredictable behaviour of low-frequency sounds had hindered the development of stereophonic recording and surround sound. Finding a way to reproduce dialogue appropriately to left and right on the movie screen had been the immediate challenge prompting British engineer Alan Blumlein to produce the first of a stream of patents in the early 1930s relating to recording, engraving, and reproduction of sounds in appropriate spatial relation. Blumlein realized that the way human ears process sounds in motion varies according to frequency; higher frequencies and shorter wavelengths producing sharper distinctions in both phase and time of arrival than lower frequencies and longer wavelengths, which tend to blur and overlap. Blumlein disagreed with the American experimental approach of recording a symphony orchestra panoramically with spaced microphones to either side

[41] Richard Toop, *Sonntags-Abschied: a Report* (Kürten, 2005).

of the conductor, reasoning that the resulting 'hole in the middle' effect was caused by out of phase low frequencies in the combined signals cancelling one another in the space between. Blumlein patented a technique of coincident recording in which left- and right-facing microphones are positioned at the same central location, but pointed in different directions: half left and half right. That way he was able to capture meaningful directional cues in shorter wavelengths while avoiding the 'hole in the middle' of internal cancellations at longer wavelengths. The defence implications of Blumlein's discoveries in acoustical rangefinding were recognized by the British military and contributed to the development of wartime sonar and radar. Lingering disagreements between European and US record companies after the war would delay the commercial launch of stereophonic audio until 1956.

A decade-long American endeavour to simulate the effect of movement of sounds in space climaxed in 1940 with the premiere of the Disney movie *Fantasia* featuring a radically new and hugely expensive system for recording and rotating selected components of a multi-channel movie soundtrack. *Fantasia* is a particularly famous example of collaboration between the US audio industry and the world of classical music, represented by conductor Leopold Stokowski and the Philadelphia Orchestra, to investigate, develop, and promote a technology ultimately to enable voices and sound effects of future movies to move independently within a virtual three-dimensional acoustic space. Stokowski and music critic Deems Taylor designed a concert programme of contrasting instrumental items and combinations, aligned with a carefully chosen visual choreography of contrasting movements and gestures including fluid motion, a whirlpool, skating on ice, floating in air, and synchronized swimming, in all amounting to an exhaustive testing regime for exhibiting the sound projection system of the future by Bell Labs and RCA.

Premiered in 1940, the now fifth-generation Fantasound system employed an automated, optically controlled system of fader management known as panning or pan-potting. The resulting movement of sound elements in space while effective remained illusory rather than real; despite its location and orientation appearing to move from speaker to speaker, a sound's internal harmonic structure did not vary dynamically in a manner consistent with real life. Each spatial movement of a particular track was controlled by a prerecorded amplitude-modulated pure tone influencing the fader level of a designated speaker or speaker group, an arrangement permitting an intricate choreography of movements to be fixed in advance and exactly reproduced on cue. A similar concept drives present-day computer-controlled faders in a modern studio mixing desk, each channel of which 'remembers' a balance engineer's manual settings and updates.

Tornado-like rotation brings the 'Danse de la Terre' of Stokowski's arrangement of Stravinsky's *Le Sacre du Printemps* to an exciting climax, accompanying a visual spectacle of battling dinosaurs. As visual plans for this episode of *Fantasia* were taking shape, Disney's animators contemplated the unusual challenge of realistically representing the movements of physical bodies of unprecedented size and weight on an appropriately massive scale. At the suggestion of staging a battle between Tyrannosaurus Rex and Triceratops, a member of the team who knew about dinosaurs observed that the Stegosaurus would make a more dramatic opponent because of the swinging action of its tail as a weapon, resembling a ball and chain with four spikes. Animating realistic actions on such a scale had never been attempted before. Compared to recent stop-motion animation of a model King Kong climbing a model Empire State building, the task of capturing the massive, deliberate actions of dinosaurs in monster scale as well as in colour would take the art and science of motion capture to a new level.

> No human being . . . had ever seen the action of a Stegosaurus's tail. . . . While we have an accurate picture of the size and shape and weight, it was not until the Disney artists combined their study of the skeletal remains with their animators' knowledge of balance and weight that anyone had an educated visualization of how these creatures might have moved.[42]

Fantasound technology worked by separately modulating the amplitude of individual tracks of a multitrack composition, causing the total audio panorama, or parts of it, to alter position or move left or right, effects to be highlighted in demonstration discs released in the late 1950s to stimulate public interest in the stereo medium. Similar effects were showcased by Philips in a remarkable sound pavilion created for the 1958 Brussels World Fair by architect Le Corbusier and assistant engineer and composer Iannis Xenakis, featuring the *Poème électronique*, a panoramic cityscape of New York in motion created on tape by Edgar Varèse.

> Remarkable effects can be obtained with the technique of *stereophony*; sounds can be made to issue from a direction where there is no sound source and by means of electronic manipulation the impression of a moving sound can be created without there being any actual movement of the source. These effects were considered, when at the end of 1956, the Philips Company of Holland discussed the sound effects for the *Electronic Poem* with Architect M. Le Corbusier. It was required that the audience should have the illusion that various sounds were in motion around them, rising and falling, coming together and moving apart again. It was also decided that the space in which

[42] John Culhane, *Walt Disney's* Fantasia (New York, 1999), p. 121.

> this took place was to seem [acoustically] 'narrow and dry' at one instance, and at another to have the reverberation of a cathedral. The final reproduction of the electronic music that was composed by Edgar Varèse was obtained from a three-track tape recording, the whole system being controlled by a second magnetic tape containing no fewer than fifteen tracks.[43]

The sound system designed by Philips technicians for the Xenakis/Le Corbusier Pavilion at the Brussels World Fair in 1958 employed a dynamic sound distribution system similar to Fantasound, but with interesting low-frequency additions.

> The acoustical effects were to be realized by means of a three-track tape, each of its synchronized tracks having its own playback head, a group of amplifiers and loudspeakers, and a multi-track machine with [amplitude modulated] signals to activate the various loudspeaker circuits. . . . The [four hundred] loudspeakers in the pavilion were divided into 'groups' and 'paths'. The groups were placed above the entrance, above the exit, and at the top of the roofs' three concavities; whereas the loudspeakers making up the paths were arranged along the ribs of the roof. A horizontal path had also been installed, and besides this there were also twenty-five large loudspeakers, behind the barrier [on the ground], for the reproduction of the deep bass range and for special effects.[44]

Unlike the *Fantasia* setup, which was designed specifically for movie theatres with seated audiences around whom the music circled, the Philips Pavilion at the Brussels World Fair was designed as a walk-through *son et lumière* experience delivering a prerecorded montage of sounds of urban New York, largely preserved in their natural state. Outstanding among a selection of robust physicality are sounds of road drills, an immense pipe organ, and a passenger jet passing overhead. The tent-like interior of the pavilion brought together a group of large-scale overhead cavities, their pleated shapes resembling the mouths of long-throw cinema loudspeakers, by means of which Philips engineers sought to create interesting acoustic illusions. A noteworthy addition was the deployment of multiple low-frequency speakers on the ground, fenced off from the public for reasons of safety (exposure to low-frequency sound can induce nausea). The choreographed distribution of sound to 400 overhead speakers was controlled by a variant of Fantasound, the entire extravaganza animated like Christmas fairy lights from sixteen channels of pre-recorded tone controls.

The benign effects of aleatoric modulation of recorded material using very low-frequency tones is addressed in Werner Meyer-Eppler's paper 'Statistic and

[43] Frederick C. Judd, *Electronic Music and Musique Concrète* (London, 1961), p. 27.

[44] Fernand Ouellette, *Edgard Varese* trans. Derek Coultman (London, 1968), pp. 199–201.

Probabilistic Problems of Sound', published in *Die Reihe I* in 1955 (and in English in 1958). An outwardly esoteric contribution to a new music periodical, the article proposed to replace the mechanical tremulant of a Lowrey electronic organ with a more natural sounding vibrato effect relying on sum and difference combinations of ultra-low-frequency tones. Within the space enclosed by a multiple speaker system such interactions create standing wave patterns causing sounds of similar wavelength to migrate towards specific locations in an acoustic effect comparable to visible Chladni patterns forming on a vibrating plate or disc.

Some expectation of this kind is implied by an otherwise obscure piece by Stockhausen, the 1952 *Schlagquartett* for piano and three pairs of timpani, an early attempt at resonance manipulation updated in 1974 as *Schlagtrio* for piano and two timpanists. The earlier quartet version, however, is significant, locating a piano in the centre of a triangle formation of three pairs of kettledrums. Strictly speaking, the arrangement postulates a shifting pattern of relationship between a central dominant instrument of variable pitch and a surrounding group of passively resonating membranes of indeterminate pitch resembling a circle of loudspeakers. Since timpani project their tone upwards, the logical way of recording or broadcasting such an ensemble in high fidelity would be to position a stereo pair of microphones relatively high over the piano with its top removed, and individual spot microphones closer to each of the three pairs of timpani, in an arrangement forming an equilateral tetrahedron. Such a formation is associated in hi-fi recording lore with the productions of the legendary Mercury Living Presence label and producer Wilma Cozart Fine. It suggests that Stockhausen's team associates and colleagues at Cologne Radio in 1952 were up to date with current developments in recording at a time when Werner Meyer-Eppler was in regular contact with Bell Labs in the United States, while Herbert Eimert was responsible for late-night new music programming at Cologne Radio, a station with an established culture of experimental recording and technical innovation.

All the same, Stockhausen's personal motive for composing *Schlagquartett* remains obscure. His published remarks on the work are few and mystical in tone. In effect what we appear to be dealing with is a transcendental metaphor for the wonder of stereo, delivered in a programme note claiming to represent the magical emergence of a new perceptual entity from the interaction of signals approaching from left and right channels, which in the act of dissolving together lose their individual identities while gaining an extra dimension in spacetime.[45] A tetrahedral arrangement of instruments and microphones suggests a work inspired by Pierre Schaeffer's 'space potentiometer' at the Club d'Essai,

[45] Stockhausen, *Stockhausen on Music*, pp. 133–5.

a Jacques Poullin designed sound projection setup allowing a controller to levitate and conduct live or pre-recorded sounds in three dimensions by theremin-like hand movements via a system of ring aerials acting upon a tetrahedral array of speakers.

Schlagquartett was premiered in 1953, withdrawn soon thereafter, and not heard again until 1974 when it reappeared on disc in rearranged form for piano and two timpanists, effectively disguising the acoustical implications of its original conception. It forms a partnership with *Kreuzspiel*, also dating from 1952, a composition in which note collections migrate towards the centre from opposite ends of the piano keyboard to collide and set in motion melodies of a plaintive character for oboe and bass clarinet. In different ways, *Schlagquartett* and *Kreuzspiel* are evidence of Stockhausen's preoccupation with a music of spatial relations from the outset of his career as a composer with Cologne Radio.

> Having studied everything, including the new Buchla synthesizers and the latest Moog developments, and also after an exchange of letters with [Peter] Zinovieff, I have decided not to recommend di Guigno's apparatus or the method already being followed at IRCAM, for Cologne. What I want is a studio set up rather like an airplane cockpit. . . . I want a machine that will simulate whatever generators, filters, or transformers I may need, and I want it to respond instantly to the physical actions of my body. . . . So what I want is analogue production, and I want any re-simulation also in analogue form, so that I can influence the parameters separately.[46]

In 1958 Stockhausen was invited by Lawrence Morton and Leonard Stein to travel to Los Angeles to conduct a concert of his music and give lectures at two universities. 'Find me a few more engagements in the United States,' the composer replied, 'and I will come in November.' Interest was such that a six-week-long itinerary was arranged, involving criss-crossing the continent to different locations in the United States and Canada. In addition to an illustrated lecture titled 'New Electronic and Instrumental Music', Stockhausen came prepared with two additional papers of more esoteric appeal: 'Music in space', on the composition of sounds moving in space, and 'Speech and music' on the analysis and resimulation of speech sounds, a subject of particular interest to Meyer-Eppler's American contacts in the artificial intelligence community. Accompanying him on tour were tapes from the Cologne studio, including his own *Electronic Studies I* and *II*, *Gesang der Jünglinge*, *Gruppen* for three orchestras, and a sampler of vocoder-influenced studies of scrambled, rotated, and reassembled speech.

[46] Maconie, *Other Planets*, pp. 82–4.

As late as 1958, public appreciation of moving sounds in space was still a minority interest. A ten-inch vinyl recording of *Gesang der Jünglinge*, Stockhausen's most celebrated achievement in speech synthesis, a composition in five-channel polyphony, had been released by Deutsche Grammophon – but only in mono. The premiere of *Gruppen* had attracted widespread attention on account of a Stan Kenton–style big band hurrah moment inserted at rehearsal number 119 towards the end of the work in which brass choruses swing back and forth among spatially separated choirs of trombones and horns. Discussion topics of recent interest included the moving sound patterns of Varèse's *Poème électronique* and the acoustics of the complicated Philips distribution system and customized sound shell of the Brussels Expo.

Stockhausen was eager to consult with American knowhow on topics relating to reverberation and techniques for moving sounds in space. These included a radical proposal by Canadian-American composer Henry Brant to record a composition for four orchestras in four-channel surround sound by recording the same orchestra four times, one after the other, each in a different corner of the same auditorium and combined on separate tracks of a four-channel tape, the composer claiming that in this way the acoustic integrity of the space would be safely preserved.[47] Earlier in 1958, in a sleeve note to accompany the release by Philips/Columbia of a recording of Stockhausen's *Zeitmasse* and Boulez's *Le marteau*, the American conductor and Stravinsky associate Robert Craft had written, 'Stockhausen's inventiveness and discovery in [the] field of rhythmic co-ordination are of the greatest interest and importance. There are, incidentally, even more striking passages of this sort in his *Gruppen* for three orchestras (which we plan to record for American Columbia in the near future, one orchestra at a time against ourselves).' That project never materialized, but for an idea so similar to Brant's to be advanced at all is curious to say the least.[48] Joan Peyser would later divulge that Brant's 1955 paper 'Uses of Antiphonal Distribution and Polyphony of Tempi in Composing' had been consulted by Stockhausen during the preparation of *Gruppen*. Among Stockhausen's list of acquisitions during his month-long US sojourn were a recording of Brant's *Galaxy 2* (1954), along with an extended article describing the Canadian-American composer's *Grand Universal Circus* (1956), a kind of happening in the spirit of John Cage.

[47] Henry Brant, 'Space as an Essential Aspect of Musical Composition'. In Elliott Schwartz and Barney Childs eds., *Contemporary Composers on Contemporary Music* (New York, 1967), pp. 223–42.

[48] Robert Craft, 'Boulez and Stockhausen', *The Score* 24 (1958), pp. 54–62.

Stockhausen's invitation to visit Los Angeles had come barely a year after Stravinsky's courtesy call to Cologne Radio in 1957, following a visit to St Mark's Basilica in Venice to record *Canticum Sacrum* for Vega, Boulez's Domaine Musical label, with Craft conducting. During his stay the venerable composer praised the work of the Cologne studio and was entertained by a seventy-fifth birthday greeting in the form of an electronic canon on the salutation 'Zu Ehren von Igor Stravinsky' voiced by director Herbert Eimert. Although only serial in parts, *Canticum Sacrum* deserves recognition as a serious contribution to the conversation on the implications of high-fidelity stereo recording and reproduction of classic antiphonal and spatial effects. Drawing inspiration from the school of Monteverdi and dedicating *Canticum Sacrum* to St Mark's, a space of multiple reverberant chapels, Stravinsky appeared to take a stand in opposition to the spatially neutralizing implications of contemporary recording practice, in effect by highlighting the roles of natural ambience, direction, and relative distance from the microphone as musically significant variables, and not just background effects over which the composer had no control.

> One of the most prominent features of San Marco is the presence of two opposing and elevated choir lofts, each with its own organ. Two large arches are visible on either side: the narrower arches locate the elevated musicians' gallery; the much larger adjacent arches locate the choir where the organs are housed. . . . The musicians could also perform from a number of places in the basilica, and on more important feasts they typically sang from one of the two elevated pulpits supported by columns just above floor level in the crossing.[49]

Canticum Sacrum is a genuine high-fidelity composition of exceptional contrasts, a work including some of Stravinsky's loudest, deepest, most dense, delicate, and extreme tone combinations of timbres and frequencies. Opening and closing choruses 'Euntes in mundum' and 'Ille autem profecti' are not only exceptionally loud and dense examples of a musical palindrome, but in the words of Glenn Watkins are 'explicitly referential – this time to the *stile concitato* or "agitated, warlike style" of Claudio Monteverdi'. Stravinsky's exceptionally expanded dynamics, density, directional, and distance effects appear designed to show empathy with new developments in parametric serialism, and – interestingly for a work destined to be recorded in mono – a special sensitivity to spatial relations as contrasting expressions of direct and reflected energies.

In Madison, Wisconsin, Stockhausen encountered pianist Gunnar Johansen (1906–91), a Busoni specialist and pianist in residence at the University of

[49] Glenn Watkins, *The Gesualdo Hex: Music, Myth, and Memory* (New York, 2010), pp. 156–7.

Wisconsin. Johansen recommended Stockhausen to contact a colleague, Charles Litton Sr., an electronics engineer with whom Johansen was collaborating on recording projects. Contemplating a free day while in San Francisco, Stockhausen called Litton to ask his advice about reverberation control. 'He knew exactly what I was talking about and offered to make the three-hour drive to San Francisco to pick me up', adding 'you won't regret it.' Reverberation had played a distinctive role in the polyphony of *Gesang der Jünglinge*, but applied intuitively in piecemeal fashion to sounds and groups. The aim was to improve and unify the quality of ambience associated with a polyphony of individual sounds, as Stravinsky had described the richly harmonious acoustic of a cathedral or basilica such as St Mark's.

An engineer and entrepreneur, Litton had made a reputation as an innovator in the region of California destined to become famous as Silicon Valley. The founder manager of a successful electronics factory making vacuum tubes for a range of civilian and defence applications, in 1953 he had sold the firm, and in 1954 the Litton brand name, relocating to the country where he continued to manufacture precision equipment, observing that after Sputnik, the days of valve technology were numbered; it was time to move into a new era of satellite communication, transistors, and circuit boards.

> 'What do you use at Cologne Radio for reverberation?' he asked. I answered, 'We have reverberation plates with preset delays'. 'Aha! I prefer adjustable tape heads, like the people at Philips.[50] Do you get any distortion with your echo plates?' 'Yes', I replied, 'but only in series [*beim Itirieren*], when the sounds become metallic'. 'I will play you a recording I just made with Gunnar Johansen'. We enter a kidney shaped room, with no corners. Hand-clap. 'Hear that? 0.3 second reverberation'. He draws a curtain covering part of one wall. A second clap. 'Now 0.1 second reverberation'. We don't need to adjust reverberation this way any more. It can all be done purely electrically'.[51]
>
> [Then] I heard the recorded sound of a piano like never before in my entire life. Piano tones suspended in the room in mid-air like spheres, invisible shimmering bodies. The whole room was filled with sound, but I had no way of knowing where the sound was coming from.[52]

Stockhausen is describing an acoustic experience associated with a flight simulator or facility for anti-aircraft artillery training or bomb aiming, involving the visual and aural projection of moving targets at high speed. Such an environment has curved walls for realistic image projection and only one

[50] Karlheinz Stockhausen, 'Musikalische Eindrücke einer Amerikareise'. In Dieter Schnebel ed. *Texte Band 2: zu eigenen Werken* (Cologne, 1964), pp. 227–9.
[51] Ibid., p. 228.
[52] Igor Stravinsky and Robert Craft, *Themes and Episodes* (New York, 1966), pp. 11–13.

'sweet spot' – the pilot's or gun operator's seat. Acoustically the three-dimensional impression that so captivated Stockhausen would appear to have relied on finely adjusted phase relations between non-coincident microphones set up at varying distances from the piano, and a similar level of precision in balancing reverberation. Alas, the demonstration, while effective, depended entirely on a unique focal point, the sweet spot occupied by a single listener; it was not designed, nor could it be engineered, to reproduce a coherent sound field in a space occupied by an audience, let alone an audience in motion.

Soon after his return to Cologne, Stockhausen made two important changes to works in progress. To the surprise and apparent dismay of copyist and chronicler Cornelius Cardew, the composer inserted rotary X-moments to the four orchestral scores of *Carré*: moments of great turbulence in which layers of granular orchestral sound are set in independent circular motion bringing a much-needed dynamism to a hitherto relatively static score originally conceived in call and answer mode. To the tape composition *Kontakte* Stockhausen introduced the rotation table, a turntable and horn assembly seemingly mounted above an upward facing speaker cabinet. In rerecording portions of tape in four channels while manually rotating the sound projection horn within a square formation of four microphones, Stockhausen aimed to introduce an element of controlled dynamic rotary motion to tape material originally designed to be spontaneously moved about in real time by fader controls operated by four performers onstage.

Inert tone mixtures of varying density and thickness had previously been tried and tested in *Electronic Studies I* and *II*; in *Carré* and *Kontakte* the sound material is distinctly more animated, containing ingredients of internal movement as well as allowing for ad lib combined fading. Each member of the original *Kontakte* cast of four players would be assigned a fader control for one of four speakers arranged in a diamond shape, north, south, east, and west. For the four orchestras of *Carré*, the four conductors were similarly to act in concert as virtual faders, raising and lowering the volume by hand gesture.

Each orchestra in *Carré* incorporates an eight-voice SATB choir 2.2.2.2 as substitute for a reduced complement of strings 4.0.2.2.0. The use of voices to replace string players is a refinement previously associated with Stravinsky's *Symphony of Psalms* (1930), a decision addressing the uncertain behaviour of microphones in the early days of radio, and in consideration of the work's terms of commission as a broadcast special event. Stravinsky's experience of this unusual choice of instrumentation, for reasons of direct interest to Stockhausen in 1958, may explain Stravinsky's reported enthusiasm for *Carré* in conversation with Robert Craft, describing the work in glowing terms as 'a good length ahead' of the earlier *Gruppen*, a work he had previously rated extremely highly.[53]

In a letter to the author, Stockhausen admitted that pan-potting trial rehearsals of *Kontakte* with the four players, each controlling the level of one channel of a diamond-shaped four-channel array, had not gone according to plan. 'The players did not know what to do.' Section III of the present score of *Kontakte*, Structure I of the original work plan, remains an example of the kind of musical material designed for the purpose: a meditative sequence of long, drawn-out sounds detonating and gliding slowly away into the distance.

The spatial interactions of *Carré*'s four orchestras conjure up a more formal impression, say, of four lions barking at one another from separate cages, or a slow-motion Sumo wrestling match over who should occupy the centre ground. Compared to the simple rotations of pre-recorded tape material in *Kontakte* the avalanches of orchestral sound unleashed in *Carré* are awe-inspiring. Both rotary processes, however, suggest that the composer's sojourn in America was a transformative experience leading Stockhausen to reject Boulez's preference for manually controlled 'adaptive timing' in favour of a more powerful machine-oriented dynamic.

As if by coincidence, in 1961 Universal Edition, Stockhausen's publisher, listed a new piece for orchestra by Richard Hoffmann, a faculty member at Oberlin College. The former professor, Arnold Schoenberg's pupil and assistant in the composer's final years, Hoffmann is one of very few US composers Stockhausen identifies by name as having met during his American tour. Among the instrumentation of Hoffmann's score, plainly titled *Orchestra Piece 1961*, is a rotating horn alarm siren of the kind employed in country towns to signal an approaching air raid or local emergency. The sweeping tones of fire sirens of a non-pivoting kind had been introduced to concert music by Edgar Varèse in 1923; on the other hand a horn rotating at the top of a pole promises to introduce an additional range of effects, most obviously periodic Doppler oscillations and amplitude fluctuations.

When sounds originating inside a sound field are reproduced from points seemingly beyond the periphery, as from a circle of loudspeakers, it is not surprising if perceptual anomalies arise. Unlike pan-potting, which is typically slow, smooth, and continuous, sounds that are rotated at speed within a spaced speaker configuration tend to break up. Flap echo is a reverberation special effect from sci-fi movie soundtracks of the 1950s. 'In general, a loop of tape is recorded on, then passed over several playback heads in succession, these being

[53] Karlheinz Stockhausen, 'Kathinkas Gesang: Composition and Realization'. Liner notes to cd *Prix Ars Electronica 90*, Austrian Radio LC 7532. *See also* Maconie, *Other Planets*, pp. 408–12.

so spaced out that a continually repeating signal is produced, so creating the effect of reverberation.'[54] The flap element arises from the rapidly moving sound issuing in a narrowly focused beam and passing rapidly from speaker to speaker so that only one speaker at a time is carrying the signal. In real-world conditions the sound created by a whirring slingshot or bull-roarer spirals continuously outward in every direction. Thirty-nine seconds into the beginning of *Kontakte* the breakup becomes audible as the electronic sound leaps from speaker to speaker. Such an effect, were it to exceed twenty repetitions a second, would give rise to a throaty, rich, low-frequency tone of sawtooth form.

The impulsive 'siren effect' of a flow of energy passing through a perforated disc in rapid rotation had previously been studied by Helmholtz in the nineteenth century as a model of the mechanism of voice production. An electronic version of the technique was adopted by Stockhausen and his assistant Gottfried Michael Koenig for tape loop experiments in waveform synthesis, starting in 1958 in preparation for *Kontakte*. Twelve years later, a hand-cranked 'tone mill' or music grinder resembling a modified Helmholtz siren became the surprisingly retro centrepiece of Stockhausen's geodesic German Pavilion at the Osaka Expo '70, a manual device employed by the composer to spin sound combinations produced spontaneously by a team of musicians, in varying directions at up to dizzying speed, presumably in the hope that the curved interior space might lead to three-dimensional illusions similar to those he had experienced at Litton's California laboratory.

Stockhausen's contrasting choice of a reverse funnel-shaped speaker for the rotating turntable of *Kontakte* was an interesting feature arguably intended to preserve Doppler shifts within the sound, reduce spill, and concentrate the directional effect to each microphone in succession. Compared to a conventional flared speaker cone, which allows a smooth expansion of pressure passing into the atmosphere, a narrowing aperture is guaranteed to introduce transient distortions which might have been avoided with a horn of more conventional design. That Stockhausen adopted a turntable arrangement of such a design for *Kontakte* suggests either that he wanted the added distortion and preferred a narrow beam of sound, or did not know what to expect. That he recognized and intended to incorporate real-life Doppler effects rather than rely on pan-potting is a more logical inference, and for that reason a choice likely to have been reached with technical advice.

For the opening and closing flying saucer arrival and departure moments of Stockhausen's *Sirius* (1977) extremely fast rotations at audible periodicities were obtained by means of a specially constructed sound turbine, and

[54] Alan Douglas, *The Electronic Musical Instrument Manual* (London, 1968), p. 150.

reproduced through a horizontal eight-channel circle of speakers surrounding the audience. At very high rotational speeds a listener within the circle is aware of static shimmering columns of sound occupying the room space, an effect subject to highly localized spontaneous variations in direction and harmonic composition in response to the slightest head movement of the individual listener. As Stockhausen observed, the sound 'starts dancing completely irregularly in the room – at the left, in front, it's everywhere' – even changing in pitch. The shimmering columns of sound experienced in *Sirius* amount to complex standing waves created from the transitory interactions of harmonic components issuing from speakers directly facing one another in direct line with the listener.

Whether the composer fully understood how the *Sirius* effect was achieved remains unclear. But he treated it as a significant discovery, and it is reasonable to suppose that part of his motivation in composing *Cosmic Pulses* was the thought of commercially available synthesizers in 2007 having evolved to a point where the rotational effects he had in mind would be available at the touch of a button or fader control. It is tempting to imagine the effect as the composer's ultimate attempt to realize an epiphany of tongues of flame similar to *Gesang der Jünglinge*, but on a richer, more immersive, intimidating, and varied scale.

In December 1983 Stockhausen travelled to Boulez's IRCAM in Paris for the first of two fortnight-long sessions of work with technical assistant Marc Battier on a computer-generated accompaniment to the solo flute work 'Kathinkas Gesang als Luzifers Requiem' (Kathinka's song as Lucifer's Requiem), Scene 2 of the opera *Samstag aus LICHT*. In a preliminary version of the piece a solo flutist costumed as a cat performs in the company of 'tin men' – mute players costumed as oversized robots or 'tinkers'. The stumbling presence of six players improvising whirring mechanical metallic sounds was the composer's intentionally sardonic reaction to the glossy electronic sonorities of IRCAM's computer, timbres seemingly inspired by the suave vibraphone choruses of Dave Brubeck–era jazz.

At this time in 1983, Boulez was poised to seal his authority in the field of electroacoustic music with the premiere of a major composition, *Répons*, for orchestra, six soloists, and computer-generated sounds, a title claiming to bring live and artificial musical intelligence face to face in real-time, quasi-improvised dialogue. The entire concept, redolent of science fiction of the fifties, appeared designed in triumphant fulfilment of Alan Turing's famous challenge, a test to determine which unseen participant in a dialogue conducted anonymously at the keyboard – or nowadays, via social media – is a real person, and which a robot intelligence. Regarded by many as Boulez's crowning achievement, *Répons* reasserted the authority of the human will with the assistance of customized software obliging the android intelligence to follow, rather than dictate, the timing cues of the living participant in the dialogue.

For the above and a host of other reasons, Stockhausen's two fortnight-long pilgrimages to IRCAM in 1983 and 1984 are open to interpretation as a gesture of grudging endorsement of IRCAM's digital technology and a long-awaited renewal of diplomatic relations with Boulez after their disagreements over the mobile form of *Momente*, and the role of ring modulation in *Mixtur*. Stockhausen's presence at IRCAM at a critical moment in the institution's history would be seen as a public gesture of endorsement. An elegant graphic by Wilhelm Bernhard Kirchgaesser (1923–2000) from the Universal Edition score of Stockhausen's *Zyklus* for solo percussionist had been chosen to grace the cover of John R. Pierce's *The Science of Musical Sounds*, a Scientific American special edition celebrating the launch of IRCAM and recognizing the contributions of Pierce and a team of former Bell Labs advisers.

The formidable task faced by Marc Battier to meet Stockhausen's demands for the new version of 'Kathinkas Gesang' involved the realization of a complex harmonious signal in rapid continuous rotation around a centre point occupied by the solo flute player. The project was based on digital samples archived at IRCAM of a selection of low-frequency tone spectra of instruments of contrasting timbres, all of which had been recorded in unprecedented high definition extending to hundreds of overtones. IRCAM engineers were particularly proud of these samples of real musical instrument tones which had been created to impress visiting fellow engineers and scientists. On this occasion, however, the rotation would assign Doppler effects specific to each individual partial tone. Stockhausen planned to take a selection of complex tones one at a time, setting each in reverse rotation so that instead of starting with a bang, the rotation process descended from the highest frequencies, eventually to terminate abruptly at its lowest point in a sequence of stunning detonations out of which lively and musically meaningful shapes would arise to converge on the solo flutist in the centre. 'The most essential aspect is the six-layered space-polyphony of controlled phase-rotations of harmonic spectra,' declared the composer.

> Simultaneous phase-rotations of phase-synchronous partial groups of rich overtone-spectra … can be of a beauty such as has never before been experienced… . One can accurately follow quarter-, third-, and above all half-phases; and the coincidence of the maxima of all of the overtones (where a sharp explosion occurs at the point of phase synchronization) is perceived each time as a liberating new beginning.[21]

The powerful image of rotational power coming to focus at a single animated figure would stand as Stockhausen's brusque rejoinder to the recherché dialogues of solo flute, midi flutes, and electronics of a glossy new version of Boulez's *Explosante–fixe* released in 1993.

Stockhausen's title 'Kathinkas Gesang' alludes to the composer's earlier *Gesang der Jünglinge*, a work in which the sound of a treble voice appears to condense out of a synthesized maelstrom of fragments of parts of speech. In the electronic version of 'Kathinkas Gesang' the flute reacts to the computer-synthesized vortex with a sequence of voice-like chirps and trills modelled on cyclical processes and gestures, perhaps intended to evoke the precisely timed but formulaic miniature figurations of a *serinette* or cuckoo-clock.

Coincidentally in 1984, the sonically promising idea of a concert event in which chorus and principal singers perform simultaneously on roller skates onstage was announced by the choreographers of Andrew Lloyd Webber's *Starlight Express*, a London production posing the interesting acoustical challenge of recording and reproducing in surround sound the multiple complexities of a system of singing players orbiting individually in different directions. In practice, the fascinating challenge of reproducing the performers' interactions acoustically was avoided by having the players wear personal radio microphones, cancelling the onstage choreography. In similar fashion, the choreography of 'Michaelion' (1997), the final scene from Stockhausen's opera *Mittwoch aus LICHT*, requires players to enter and depart, sing, spin and orbit independently and with somewhat greater decorum to a scrupulously notated script; here too the acoustical challenges of accurately reproducing the totality of movements electronically or in recorded form remain largely unresolved.

Many of Stockhausen's formal exercises in static and dynamic spatialization are prefigured in accounts of experiments conducted by Henry Brant at Bennington College in the 1950s; among Stockhausen's later operas are choreographies of slower and more stately processions in medieval style, in designs seemingly patterned after the topographically contoured imagery of the artist Friedensreich Hundertwasser. Stockhausen had come rather late to the idea of choreographed motion on a human scale with *Harlekin* for solo clarinet (1975), a work in which nature once again imitates technology, the solo clarinet spinning and whirling in a vain endeavour to reproduce on a human scale the dazzling effect of *Sirius*'s eight-channel electronic tornado. Linear and rotational movements on a reduced scale feature in the solo flute of 'Kathinkas Gesang' and *en masse* in 'Luzifers Abschied' from *Samstag aus LICHT*; become diagonal and vertical in scenes of combat and air defence from *Dienstag aus LICHT*, and revert to graceful spiral formations in choir scenes from *Sonntag aus LICHT*. Needless to say, all such examples of musical choreography present a challenge to record producers, balance engineers, and systems designers.

Cosmic Pulses is the final chapter of a sequence of studies pursued throughout a composing life motivated by atom-splitting ideas of breaking down and reforming timbres, moving sounds in space, and delving into the inner structures and universal laws governing the cycles of natural phenomena from galaxies in the cosmos to subatomic particles blinking in and out of existence. From one perspective *Cosmic Pulses* can be interpreted as the final act of an aggrieved disciple of Goethe flushing all of Empiricist science and technology, including Newton's universe, down the toilet. While the relatively crude tonal material and lack of variety or finish of *Cosmic Pulses* compared to *Kontakte* or 'Kathinkas Gesang' are indicators of genuine haste, the resulting absence of distracting aesthetic qualities also has the positive effect of focusing attention on outstanding technical issues of the kind previously posed by Stockhausen's *Mikrophonie I*, the *Indianerlieder*, and *Mixtur*. Lingering questions of taste tell us only that the composer is not trying to score glamour points for colour or style. What remains incompletely resolved is the appropriate presentation of a schema of multiple rotations at speeds up to and including audible frequencies, and ranging in pitch over seven octaves from the lowest humanly audible tones to well in excess of 5,000 Hertz, beyond the human range of pitch discrimination. These composite cycles of speaker rotations and their interactions form the intellectual core of *Cosmic Pulses*. For a single sound mass in rapid rotation among a circle of eight speakers, as in *Sirius*, the sound will inevitably break up, although interesting results are obtained. But when multiple rotations of mid- to high-tone sequences at audio speeds are distributed by design among partial and unevenly spaced selections of three, four, or six speakers out of a total array of eight, breaks in continuity of flow are certain to be more pronounced. While solutions are conceivable, the present version of *Cosmic Pulses* is not one of them. It is as if the composer were making a last-ditch effort to harness digital processing to achieve results that had eluded him in the analogue domain. His reported misgivings as to whether the work should be called *music* or merely a sketch only reinforce that conclusion.

Music Since 1945

About the Series

Elements in Music Since 1945 is a highly stimulating collection of authoritative online essays that reflects the latest research into a wide range of musical topics of international significance since the Second World War. Individual Elements are organised into constantly evolving clusters devoted to such topics as art music, jazz, music and image, stage and screen genres, music and media, music and place, immersive music, music and movement, music and politics, music and conflict, and music and society. The latest research questions in theory, criticism, musicology, composition and performance are also given cutting-edge and thought-provoking coverage. The digital-first format allows authors to respond rapidly to new research trends, with contributions being updated to reflect the latest thinking in their fields, and the essays are enhanced by the provision of an exciting range of online resources.

Cambridge Elements

Music Since 1945

Elements in the Series

Music Transforming Conflict
Ariana Phillips-Hutton

Herbert Eimert and the Darmstadt School: The Consolidation of the Avant-Garde
Max Erwin

Baroque Music in Post-War Cinema: Performance Practice and Musical Style
Donald Greig

A Semiotic Approach to Open Notations: Ambiguity as Opportunity
Tristan McKay

Film Music in Concert: The Pioneering Role of the Boston Pops Orchestra
Emilio Audissino

Theory of Prominence: Temporal Structure of Music Based on Linguistic Stress
Bryan Hayslett

Understanding Stockhausen
Robin Maconie

A full series listing is available at: www.cambridge.org/em45

Printed in the United States
by Baker & Taylor Publisher Services